TIME OF GRACE®

A Devotional Companion

By MARK JESKE

Concordia Publishing House • Saint Louis

Published by Concordia Publishing House
3558 S. Jefferson Avenue, St. Louis, MO 63118-3968
1-800-325-3040 • www.cph.org

Manufactured in the United States of America

Library of Congress Cataloging-in-Publication Data

Jeske, Mark A.
Time of grace : a devotional companion / by Mark Jeske.
p. cm.
ISBN 978-0-7586-1913-6
1. Christian life--Biblical teaching. 2. Bible--Devotional literature.
3. Devotional calendars. I. Title.
BS600.C47J47 2010
242'.2--dc22
2010001383

1 2 3 4 5 6 7 8 9 10 19 18 17 16 15 14 13 12 11 10

Foreword

Therefore, since brevity is the soul of wit,
and tediousness the limbs and outward flourishes,
I will be brief.

There is a delicious irony in these words. They were uttered in *Hamlet*, act 2, by Polonius, one of the biggest windbags in all of Shakespeare. Still, it's the truth. Brevity is indeed the soul of wit. Mark Twain was probably right when he ventured the opinion that not many souls were saved after the first twenty minutes in a sermon.

These little daily devotions are probably the most popular of *Time of Grace's* pieces of literature. I'm sure it's because they're short. The first batches of them arose as one-minute radio scripts, and they have since been pressed into service as monthly devotional booklets, Web-site devotions, and daily e-mails.

I call them "Bible studies for busy people." It is my hope that these little nuggets of God's Word will soothe your soul and give you encouragement and hope for tomorrow. The dominant theme is *grace*—the amazing promise of Scripture that God chooses to love unlovely people "That they might lovely be," if I may be permitted to quote from Samuel Crossman's sweet hymn (*LSB* 430:1).

I would like to dedicate this book to Bruce Eberle, my friend and inspiration, who is the father of *Time of Grace*.

Mark A. Jeske
Autumn 2009

JANUARY

The Lord make
His face to shine upon you
and be gracious to you.

Numbers 6:25

January 1, New Year's Day

Forgiveness, Not Payback

It's hard to forgive. I know. I am still holding onto some old, painful memories as though they were treasury bonds. But I know this, and I want you to know it too: refusing to forgive those who have hurt you will only make you emotionally (and maybe physically) sick.

Refusal to forgive keeps you trapped in an anger prison. Refusal to forgive leads to a false sense of moral superiority. Refusal to forgive poisons and embitters your spirit. Refusal to forgive motivates Christ to withhold the forgiveness you need (yeah, seriously—check out Matthew 6:15).

Want to start off the New Year right? Here's a better way. Fill your soul with joyful praise to your forgiving Savior. Fill your heart with the same spirit He shows you: **"[Bear] with one another and, if one has a complaint against another, [forgive] each other; as the Lord has forgiven you, so you also must forgive"** (Colossians 3:13). And know this: no matter how hard that may seem, the Lord will always give you the strength to do what is right.

January 2

Pain Has Limits Set by God

One of our recurring fantasies is to be like some people who seem to have it all, who have no problems, who just seem to cruise through life. You can see their faces and hear their stories on prime-time TV. Maybe you wish you could have a life like theirs.

Maybe you've secretly wished you could be a Christian superhero like Abraham or David or Paul. Actually, the heroes of the Bible suffered as much as or more than you do.

One of the great sources of inspiration that helped Paul was God's promise to set limits to the amount of pain he would have to endure. Paul rejoiced to know that God would not let him be squeezed beyond what he could handle. God has set limits for each of us, that our troubles may go only so far and no more. Paul wrote to some struggling Christians long ago, and he says to you now, **"We are afflicted in every way, but not crushed; perplexed, but not driven to despair; persecuted, but not forsaken; struck down, but not destroyed"** (2 Corinthians 4:8–9).

Hey—cheer up!

January 3

God Explains Things to Me

Does Christianity seem logical to you? You know, quite a few features of the Gospel message are puzzles. Isn't it the essence of justice that the guilty should be punished and the innocent set free?

But God approved that Jesus Christ, the innocent, should be put to a cruel death, while we guilty sinners should be forgiven. How could one Man's actions two thousand years ago be the difference between life and death for me today?

Does any of this make sense to you? It does if the Holy Spirit is helping you understand. The Bible says in 1 Corinthians 2:9–10, **"'What no eye has seen, nor ear heard, nor the heart of man imagined, what God has prepared for those who love Him'—these things God has revealed to us through the Spirit."**

The Holy Spirit is working in you. Are you listening?

JANUARY 4

Just Looking

Some people assume that pornography was more or less invented by *Playboy* magazine. Actually, many of the very first photographic images made, in the years before the Civil War, had sexual content. Why? For the money, of course. Sex always sells.

Today we are awash in it. Most corner gas stations and truck stops have plastic-covered magazines on the top shelf. Some estimate that 30 percent of all Web sites are pornographic. Does it matter? Is it really adultery if you're just looking?

The Lord Jesus Himself, who had to endure Satan's sexual temptation just as much as we do, warned that sin is not only in the action but in the thought process as well: **"I say to you that everyone who looks at a woman with lustful intent has already committed adultery with her in his heart"** (Matthew 5:28).

Jesus has forgiven your sexual sins, including your sinful thoughts. And His Spirit works in you to live a pure life. Husbands, look at your wives. Single women, put your energy into finding a good husband. You can trust Jesus to tell you how to be truly happy and satisfied.

January 5

Parents Build Up Their Families

Do you get braggy Christmas letters from friends and relatives? They're pretty hard to take, aren't they? I don't know if the writers are bragging more about their spectacular children or boasting about what fabulous parents they are.

But the reverse is worse—parents who belittle their children, expect them to fail, or are so perfectionistic that nothing is ever good enough for them. Single moms and dads have an additional peril to overcome: how do you not take out your frustration over the missing parent on the kids?

One of the greatest gifts parents can give their kids is unconditional love and acceptance, just as our Savior loves and accepts us. Jesus' Gospel promises acceptance-based performance, not performance-based acceptance. Parents, watch your mouths. Ephesians 4:29 says, **"Let no corrupting talk come out of your mouths, but only such as is good for building up, as fits the occasion, that it may give grace to those who hear."**

Is there a child in your life whom you can build up today? Pick up the phone. Do it now.

January 6

Together with the Saints

This is the day that commemorates the visit of Gentile Magi to the infant Savior's cradle. You know, Jesus' birth in the animal shed was a pretty lonely event. Mary and Joseph probably had only animal company when Jesus arrived on earth. I'm sure they were mightily encouraged by the Magi visit some time later.

Do you ever get lonely? Do you ever feel isolated? Do you sometimes feel unloved and unappreciated? Perhaps you're singing those lonesome blues right now. If so, celebrate with me today one of the best things about God's gift of eternal life with Him in heaven: we will be surrounded by kind, wonderful people who will care about us.

The apostle John was given a preview of heaven. He wrote in Revelation 7:9, **"I looked, and behold, [I saw] a great multitude that no one could number, from every nation, from all tribes and peoples and languages, standing before the throne and before the Lamb [Jesus], clothed in white robes,"** that is, the covering of holiness that all believers receive from Jesus.

Some people hate going to funerals because it reminds them of yet another loss. I like to think that each death of a believer only means that there will be more and more friends for me when I finally enter eternal life.

I can't wait.

JANUARY 7

Look Up!

Mondays can be tough, can't they? Monday, October 19, 1987, was especially bad. On Wall Street, they called it "Black Monday" because the stock market crash that day was the largest in history. Twenty-two percent of the worth of the Dow Jones stocks evaporated in a matter of hours.

When pieces of your world are crashing, take just a minute and remember what God did for you on the very first Monday in human history—He created the sky. **"God said, 'Let there be an expanse in the midst of the waters, and let it separate the waters from the waters.' And God made the expanse and separated the waters that were under the expanse from the waters that were above the expanse. And it was so. And God called the expanse Heaven"** (Genesis 1:6–8). Our lovely planet is surrounded by a blue canopy filled with things we need: warmth, oxygen, and moisture.

If your day isn't so hot, stop looking down. Go outside and look up. Marvel at God's creative wisdom and skill. God must really love people to make something so useful and beautiful. It's the same love of God for people that moved Him to secure a new heaven and new earth for those who trust in Jesus.

Resurrection Reality

What is your most miserable funeral memory? Was it burying your husband? your mom? one of your children? You know, death is always ugly. Even when one of my loved ones has passed away after a long life and lengthy illness, it still hurts to let go. Death seems so final, so cruel.

Only Jesus Christ has a rescue from the grave. He instructed the prophet Daniel to inform us, **"Many of those who sleep in the dust of the earth shall awake"** (Daniel 12:2). I think I can bear almost anything, knowing that my Savior will catch me when I fall. I can survive any separation, knowing that I will be reunited with all believers. Those who die in the Lord aren't lost. They only get to the finish line a little before we do.

Our Lord Jesus Himself demonstrated how resurrection of the body will work. His rising authorizes Him to perform mine. And yours. My Redeemer lives. Yours does too.

Man's Best Friend

You don't have to live out in the middle of a Nevada desert to be lonely. In fact, some of the loneliest people in the world are jammed into big cities, surrounded by people, surrounded by strangers, isolated. Have you ever felt sad because everybody else seems to have it all—lots of friends, a decent boyfriend, children, a place to go on Thanksgiving and Christmas?

Has your birthday ever come and gone and nobody noticed? Is your phone too silent? Does it seem as though everybody around you is too busy to pay any attention to you?

Your best Friend is always there for you. Jesus said to the believers in Matthew 28:20, **"Behold, I am with you always, to the end of the age."** He is always listening, always interceding for you, always helping, always protecting.

And you know what? If you have Jesus as your friend, all the other things you need, including friends, will fall into place.

Christ Heals All Wounds

There are times when life really seems good—but then reality crashes in. Why is it that so many aspects of human life are so sick? Why must people be so cruel, jealous, crabby, embittered, and racist to one another?

Have you been wounded by the carelessness or cruelty of someone else? Or worse—is there someone in your life or in your past whom *you* have hurt?

Jesus Christ came to our sick world to help us find healing in Him. Through the forgiveness that He brings, the healing begins. As we experience God's truly unconditional love, we can learn to give that kind of love to other people. We can even learn to like ourselves again.

St. John was allowed to see what life would be like in heaven, a place where we will finally be rid of sickness and hurts altogether. In Revelation 22:2, he describes the life that is waiting for you: **"On either side of the river [stood] the tree of life with its twelve kinds of fruit, yielding its fruit each month. The leaves of the tree were for the healing of the nations."**

JANUARY 11

Your Enemy Is a Lion

One of the delicious thrills of going to the zoo is seeing ferocious wild animals in cages. We see them stalk around, glaring and growling, but we know that the steel bars make them helpless to hurt us. Still, we shiver a little when we imagine what it might be like to meet a lion on the open savanna—when he is hungry and we are the prey.

God wants you to know that your archenemy, Satan, is like a lion, and you are being stalked. The apostle Peter wrote this to some confused Christians: **"Your adversary the devil prowls around like a roaring lion, seeking someone to devour"** (1 Peter 5:8).

Satan lost his damning power over you when you came to faith in Christ. But he wants you back on death row. And because he is still the prince of this world and has great power, he will come at you again and again with pain or pleasures to persuade you to give up on God. When your own strength seems small, you can put your trust in the One who promised that no one can rip you out of His hands (John 10:28).

The Lord Jesus, the lion of the tribe of Judah, is an even bigger lion, and He has final control of all that happens in our universe. His roar is good news for us, for it is the roar of God's triumph over evil.

January 12

You Are Precious to Him

One of the greatest of all human fears is that nobody really loves us much. Have you ever suspected that the kind words you were hearing from somebody were phony? Do you ever have moments of self-doubt? Have you been lied to by someone you thought liked you?

Children are especially vulnerable to words that make them feel worthless. It is one of a parent's most important jobs to give their children an absolutely secure feeling that they are worth a lot. Children who have never been given a feeling of self-worth can become adults who can't truly love others because they hate themselves.

One profession of love you will never have to doubt is God's. God says in Jeremiah 31:3, **"I have loved you with an everlasting love; therefore I have continued My faithfulness to you."** The willing death of His Son, Jesus, proves how precious you are to Him. Jesus' death was not merely a gesture. It was the great single act that restores our broken relationship with God. The blood of Jesus shed on the cross was the very blood of God.

You matter that much to God.

January 13

Lonely in Marriage

Being married means that your best friend will always be there for you, right? Your partner will always be supportive and understanding, always ready to listen and help. Or not. It is amazing how lonely marriage can be when two people have not been taking care of the relationship. The marriage license and ceremony don't guarantee living happily ever after.

Marriage is way better than single people think, but it is also much more work. Wives who expect their husbands to read their minds and husbands who don't listen slowly push each other away. Untreated hurts make one-time lovers withdraw; the loneliness grows.

God has a better way. He came to seek us, to bridge the gap. He values us so much that He made the supreme effort by humbling Himself on the cross. He expects no less of us in the way we treat one another, especially in our own homes. Paul said, **"Be kind to one another, tenderhearted, forgiving one another, as God in Christ forgave you"** (Ephesians 4:32).

What is one thing you can do today to make your spouse's life better?

God Controls the Heavens

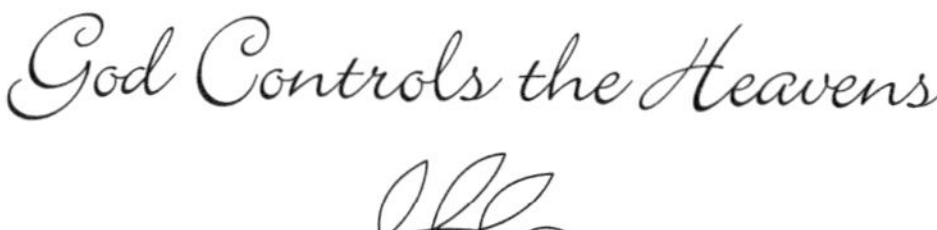

Does your world ever seem out of control? When it does, look up at the night sky. There you will see billions of stars—flaming, fiery, giant gas balls that God placed there to decorate the sky for rich and poor alike. In one of his poems, King David wrote, **"The heavens declare the glory of God, and the sky above proclaims His handiwork"** (Psalm 19:1).

What's more, God still retains total control over the heavenly bodies. The Bible tells us that God stopped the rotation of the earth for Joshua (Joshua 10:13–14) and even made it go backward for Hezekiah (2 Kings 20:9–11). Now *that's* control!

This is the God who tells you that nothing—no force in all the universe—can come between you and His love for you in Christ.

JANUARY 15

Greed

Maybe you've heard of the "seven deadly sins." According to the list of serious sins formalized by Pope Gregory I (circa AD 600), greed is number 3, outranked only by lust and gluttony. You could argue that all sins are deadly (true) and that there are far more than merely seven (true). Still, that ancient list shows a sad experience with universal human corruption. People easily fall in love with their stuff.

Or with the stuff they expect to get or wish to get. **"Whoever hastens to be rich will not go unpunished"** (Proverbs 28:20). I can spot materialism far more quickly in other people than I can in myself. But that's an excuse. There is greed in my heart too.

Any talking about the Bible's view of money must start with the common human sin of greed—that is, craving money's power, influence, and security. A spiritually healthy attitude about money must recognize greed for the disease that it is and repent of it. Only through Christ's forgiveness can the healing begin. **"Riches do not profit in the day of wrath, but righteousness delivers from death"** (Proverbs 11:4).

What do you love? Whom do you love? We love Jesus because He first loved us.

January 16

The Burden of Prosperity

You can understand and even sympathize with people whose poverty and hardships have made them suspicious of God's love and power. Has it ever occurred to you that prosperity is an even greater spiritual burden?

Jesus once told His shocked disciples, **"It is easier for a camel to go through the eye of a needle than for a rich person to enter the kingdom of God"** (Matthew 19:24). He said this from sad experience, because His encounters with the wealthy were usually not pleasant. God gives money to people as a tool to make *His* agenda happen. He provides treats because He is kind and loves to see us happy. Alas, money can easily become a god to be pursued and worshiped for the power it gives.

Has God tested you with prosperity? Is your life quite comfortable? Too comfortable? Do you struggle with trusting God because you don't have to? Do you forget to pray because right now you have more money than you need and you feel fine? Do you feel a need for God?

God has fulfilled all our needs in Christ Jesus. The riches of a new life in Him are worth more than all the possessions in the world.

January 17

Put Your Hope in God

Everybody gets depressed now and then. Some of you reading this, though, have lived through some l-o-n-g stretches of emotional misery. Depression is a fog that warps and distorts our view of reality. When those foul moods descend, you can't see anything good, any reason for hope, any love or kindness coming your way. Depressed people's loneliness gets even worse because at times like that, they aren't particularly fun to be with, and so friends drift away.

Key insight: the sad conclusions you draw when you are depressed are wrong. The reasoning is faulty, and the evil driving force behind them is Satan. Here's the truth: your Savior loves you and values you—permanently, unconditionally, and completely. Connected to Christ by faith, even a weak faith, you are never hopeless. You are always forgiven.

Psalm 43:5 has marvelous words of encouragement: **"Why are you cast down, O my soul, and why are you in turmoil within me? Hope in God; for I shall again praise Him, my salvation and my God."**

The bloody cross and the empty tomb have the power to turn depression into joy. God promises it. Claim it.

God Couldn't Love You More

Most of us don't associate pain with love. In other words, if we think somebody's hurting us, we automatically assume there's no love there. Now, if you are hurting in your life and know that God is either sending or allowing that pain, you may be tempted to cry out, "God, don't You love me anymore?"

God couldn't love you more. The Bible says in Romans 8:32, **"He who did not spare His own Son but gave Him up for us all, how will He not also with Him graciously give us all things?"** That is God's ultimate show of love.

Some of the "all things" He promises, which demonstrate His love daily, include the following: Our pain is temporary. Nothing in all the world can make Him stop loving you. Both your treats and your hardships will work for you to strengthen your faith and build spiritual stamina. After a season of trouble, He always sends relief.

January 19

Your Personal Savior

Are you one of those people who hears the stories of the amazing person and work of Jesus Christ, who marvels at His love and victories, but who fears that all those good things must be for somebody else? Do you have trouble believing and trusting that the great benefits of salvation in Christ could really apply to you? I mean, to you *personally*?

It is for just such fears that the Lord sets a table and invites you. Come to His Meal! People don't eat with enemies; they eat with friends. Jesus is your *friend* now. In fact, at His Feast, He is both host and the main course. In His Holy Supper, you encounter Christ Jesus, Lord of all, in an intensely personal way. As you receive His true body and blood, He is bonded to you and you to Him—personally! Yes, you! Little, sinful, unworthy you!

Here is His promise, the gift of Christ Himself: **"The cup of blessing that we bless, is it not a participation in the blood of Christ? The bread that we break, is it not a participation in the body of Christ?"** (1 Corinthians 10:16). There can be but one conclusion: "Jesus, You must mean me too—me personally!"

January 20

The Lord Goes with You

So tell me—what are you afraid of? Oh, come on now, don't be ashamed to admit it. Everybody has fears. Kids do too, of course. One of the deepest childhood fears is abandonment. This may seem funny to adults. When we take small children shopping, they tug and yank at our handholds, trying to break free. But when they get the freedom they want and turn around a few moments later and we aren't there, they panic.

You know, we yank on God's arms too, chafing at His limits. And sometimes He lets us have our way, running far from His side. What terrible damage we can do to people's lives, and to our own, when we no longer guide our lives with His Word!

And then comes the terror—we have gone too far, offended Him once too often, committed the unforgivable sin. What if He gives us what we deserve and abandons us?

Perhaps you feel a gap between you and God right now. Here is good news for all spiritual runaways: God's love is unconditional because it comes to us through Christ. His arms are always wide open for lost children who want to come home. Deuteronomy 31:6 tells us, **"It is the Lord your God who goes with you. He will not leave you or forsake you."**

Developing Perseverance

Here's a true-or-false quiz for you today. Ready? Okay, true or false: if you are really struggling with major issues in your life, God must be angry with you. Well, that is totally false. We live in a broken and dying world, and everybody suffers. We are victims of the cruelty of others, and sometimes we are victims of our own stupidity or greed.

But this pain that we suffer can actually serve a good purpose when it compels us to see how much we need God for forgiveness and for protection.

The apostle James wrote, **"Count it all joy, my brothers, when you meet trials of various kinds, for you know that the testing of your faith produces steadfastness"** (James 1:2–3).

Huh? Life's hardships a joy? What? You heard the man. Everybody knows you don't build tight abs with Krispy Kremes. In the same way, spiritual stamina, toughness, and resilience are formed by going through hardships and overcoming. We can do all this through Christ, who gives us the strength.

January 22

Jesus Knows Your Troubles

"I know just how you feel." Has anybody ever said that to you? Have you ever wanted to lash back, "You have no idea how this feels!"? Have you ever felt the pain of the old spiritual that says, "Nobody knows the trouble I've seen; nobody knows my sorrow"?

Jesus knows your troubles. He experienced your pain. The prophet Isaiah wrote of Jesus, **"Surely He has borne our griefs and carried our sorrows. . . . He was wounded for our transgressions; He was crushed for our iniquities; upon Him was the chastisement that brought us peace, and with His stripes we are healed"** (Isaiah 53:4–5).

The best part is, not only did Jesus know our troubles; by His actions, He *ended* them.

January 23

Heaven

It seems to me that there is a terrible amount of misinformation out there, even among Christians, about what heaven will be like. Some think we will be like the angels. (Wrong! They are spirits; we will have physical bodies.) Some think we will be up in the sky, sitting on the clouds. (Wrong! We will walk upon the new earth that the Creator will create.) Some think that we will be reincarnated for another go-round on earth. (Wrong! We will be raised once from the dead with our bodies and personalities intact and then live forever with the Lamb.)

And some people think that heaven will be ten trillion years of vacation, where we will just lie around and do nothing, being waited on forever and ever. (Wrong! We will have work to do in God's new world, work that will be pure, joyful service.) **"No longer will there be any curse. The throne of God and of the Lamb will be in the city, and His servants will serve Him. They will see His face"** (Revelation 22:3–4 NIV).

God knows that the greatest satisfaction in one's heart comes from accomplishment, not from being pampered. Perhaps Bach will write more great music, King David more great poems, and C. S. Lewis more great books. God will let you know what He needs you to do. Know this: serving the Lamb who once served you will be the greatest thrill of your eternity.

The Gift of Friends

Long-running sitcoms like *Cheers* and *Friends* were built around an aching human need: to have friends. God has wired the human spirit for community; it is not good for us to be alone.

1 Samuel 18:1 says, **"The soul of Jonathan was knit to the soul of David, and Jonathan loved him as his own soul."** The Lord knew that David, the anointed future king of Israel, was going to have to face bitter years of exile and hardship. One of the ways God helped him was to send him a great and true friend—Prince Jonathan.

How are you doing right now? Are you weary? confused? lonely? Look around you today. Some of the faces you see are God's gifts to you, gifts of friends. Listen to them. Believe their words of affection and concern. Treasure them. And don't forget that your best Friend in heaven loves you the most.

January 25

Our Time of Grace

The Joseph Schlitz Brewing Company, may it rest in peace, used to sell beer with the ad slogan "You only go around once in life, so grab for all the gusto you can." The idea was that you get only one chance to enjoy yourself, and then come death, oblivion, and nothingness.

The Bible actually tells us the opposite. We have indeed been given lives to enjoy God's goodness here on earth. But it gets better—Jesus has opened up the doors to heaven. He says, **"I came that they may have life and have it abundantly"** (John 10:10). Whoever trusts and believes in Him will actually get to go around *twice* in life.

Right now is our time of grace, a time to discover and cherish both earthly and eternal blessings. Let's be sure we don't settle for less and enjoy only what this earth has to offer before our short time here ends and God's eternity begins. *Now* is the time to repent. *Now* is the time to believe. *Now* is the time to praise.

JANUARY 26

Immanuel: God with Us

Does it ever bother you that you are invited to worship a God you can't see? If there really is a divine Maker of this world, why doesn't He hang around to let us get to know Him? God's seeming absence from this planet has led some to fear that we are all alone here and that there is nobody and nothing greater than man.

Ah, but that's not so. The Bible says that **"in [Christ] the whole fullness of deity dwells bodily"** (Colossians 2:9). Think of it—God Himself actually took on human flesh and entered our lives. The prophet Isaiah says that the child born through a wondrous virgin birth should be called Immanuel, which in Hebrew means "God is with us."

Next time you feel isolated and alone, fearful that nobody is listening when you pray, just whisper, "Immanuel!" That will help you remember, "God, You are right here with us!"

January 27

Our Heavenly Father Is Always Listening

"You're not listening to me!" For centuries, these angry words have been shouted by fearful wives at their clueless husbands. Wives are absolutely certain about this central truth: "If you love me, you will listen to me."

This is also true of our relationship with God. Since we cannot hold a back-and-forth conversation with God directly, we often grow fearful that we are all alone and that God is not listening to our prayers.

The Israelite slaves in Egypt probably figured that their God had abandoned them. But here's what was really going on: **"The Lord said, 'I have surely *seen* the affliction of My people who are in Egypt and have *heard* their cry because of their taskmasters. I *know* their sufferings, and I have come down to deliver them out of the hand of the Egyptians'"** (Exodus 3:7–8, italics added).

The key to our confidence is Jesus. Through our faith in Him, His Father is now our Father, one who has accepted the obligation of true fatherhood for us all. He sees. He hears. He cares.

The Ultimate Survivors

Are you a fan of reality TV? *Survivor*-type shows certainly have been the hottest item on the small screen in recent years. The more extreme the experience that the poor victims have to undergo, the better the audiences like it—eating worms, cuddling with snakes, jungle treks, desert hunger, miserable weather, and on and on.

The ultimate survivor experience is yet to come, and everyone living at that time will have to go through it. I speak, of course, of the Day of Judgment. The prophets tell us of the terror that people will feel when they see our universe coming apart. Even megacatastrophe movies seen in theaters with threshold-of-pain audio effects cannot adequately prepare people for the disintegration of everything that once seemed solid and dependable.

The prophets tell us also to relax and trust that our Savior will bring us through that awe-filled day. **"The sun shall be turned to darkness, and the moon to blood, before the great and awesome day of the LORD comes. And it shall come to pass that everyone who calls on the name of the LORD shall be saved"** (Joel 2:31–32).

You have Jesus. That makes you the ultimate survivor. You are safe.

JANUARY 29

Summoned by God

Are you a career person? Is all of your self-esteem caught up in your position? Does your sense of self-worth depend on your achievements? Do you fear being judged a failure in what you do?

Have you ever gotten a bad performance review? been laid off? been fired? Question: What's worse than a miserable life? Answer: A miserable eternity.

How can we be sure that we have God's approval on our lives? Here's the beauty of the Gospel: God's approval is based not on our performance, but on *His* choice and *His* redeeming work. In Isaiah 43:1–3, He assures us, **"Fear not, for I have redeemed you; I have called you by name, you are Mine. . . . I am the LORD your God, the Holy One of Israel, your Savior."** Or as St. Paul puts it, it is a gift, not wages.

Hey! Don't you feel better already?

January 30

The Spirit Encourages Me

We all sing the blues sometimes. What's in your blues song this week? dumped? betrayed? broke? hung over? robbed? hopeless?

It's hard to lift yourself out of the blues. Satan wants to keep you down, whispering "Loser!" in your ears. That's why God sends us friends, whose words of praise or comfort can help us back on our feet. He also sends us people who remind us and teach us more about Him—pastors, teachers, Bible study leaders.

The ultimate comforting friend is God the Holy Spirit. When I am plagued by doubts—especially the worst of all doubts, the doubt that God loves me—the Spirit reminds me of the Calvary love of Christ, our Savior. He helps me believe that such a great treasure can actually be mine, that heaven can actually be my destination too.

The Bible says, **"The Spirit Himself bears witness with our spirit that we are children of God, and if children, then heirs—heirs of God and fellow heirs with Christ"** (Romans 8:16–17). In the Spirit, you've got a friend. In your God, you've got a Father.

Flee Adultery

It might seem pointless to try to advocate for celibacy among single people in the twenty-first century. It might seem like a battle long lost. Do it anyway. It's never too late to relearn God's ways. If even one heart is changed, if even one life is blessed, it's worth it.

Even while tolerating and encouraging sexual behavior outside of marriage, all societies know that there are social and personal costs to it. Inconvenient pregnancies and sexually transmitted diseases are just two. God knows of those costs and more, for it was He who designed marriage as the exclusive place for human sexuality.

He guided St. Paul to write, **"Flee from sexual immorality. Every other sin a person commits is outside the body, but the sexually immoral person sins against his own body"** (1 Corinthians 6:18).

Whose word and ways can you trust more than God's? He who sent His own Son as a sacrificial lamb to take away the sin of the world isn't going to promote behaviors that will hurt us. The things He forbids really are destructive and painful. His will is good; His commandments protect precious things. Like marriage. Like your body.

February

There is therefore now
no condemnation for those
who are in Christ Jesus.

Romans 8:1

February 1

Setting Priorities

You have a priority system, whether you realize it or not. Your internal value system helps you decide what to do and which things to do first. Some people do whatever makes them feel good . . . or whatever builds up their egos . . . or whatever is easiest . . . or whatever leads to money. And you?

God claims first rights as your Creator. He bought you back from the slavery of sin and claims you all over again as your Redeemer and Savior. The washing of your Baptism put His claim on you and His Spirit in you.

There's a reason why the very first commandment on God's list instructs us to put Him first. One of the most authentic ways we can show that we have no other gods, that the Lord our God really is our number one, is to make Him the decisive factor in all major decisions.

Jesus not only encouraged that kind of thinking, but He attached a huge promise to it: **"Seek first the kingdom of God and His righteousness, and all these things will be added to you"** (Matthew 6:33). Do you believe Him? Why not give Him a try?

February 2

You Have God's Powerful Spirit

When your life gets hard and you feel overwhelmed, you can tell yourself, "Well, at least I don't have it as tough as Zerubbabel." He was the governor of Judea whose monumental task it was to rebuild the shattered nation after the Babylonian armies' terrible destruction and after seventy years of neglect and abandonment. Judea was burned, broken, and choked with weeds.

Zerubbabel was all too aware that he lacked both the people and resources to do this impossible job. The prophet Zechariah was commissioned to remind Zerubbabel that God always equips the people He calls: **"This is the word of the Lord to Zerubbabel: Not by might, nor by power, but by My Spirit, says the Lord of hosts"** (Zechariah 4:6).

Do you know what that means for you? Since the Spirit is living in you, you have greater strength than you think. You are wiser than you think. You know what else? Zerubbabel got the temple rebuilt.

February 3

Struggles Keep Me Looking Ahead

Ever been to a Little League game or a junior high basketball game and seen parents go ballistic? As they curse the refs and berate the coaches, you just want to go up to them and say, "Hey, calm down! It's just a game!"

In love, God lets us struggle and suffer sometimes so that we don't become too emotionally attached to this world. He wants us to realize that we're only camping here, just passing through. Here's His master plan: to patch us up; keep us moving along; and then, ultimately, to re-create an entirely new universe, and to remake us as well. The things that are getting you so upset? In the grand scheme of things, *it's just a game*!

Thanks to our Savior, Jesus, our real life lies ahead in the future. Soon He will take us to this new heavenly home, a place without suffering, tears, or dying. Paul rejoiced to be able to comfort troubled souls like you and me with this promise: **"This light momentary affliction is preparing for us an eternal weight of glory beyond all comparison, as we look not to the things that are seen but to the things that are unseen. For the things that are seen are transient, but the things that are unseen are eternal"** (2 Corinthians 4:17–18).

February 4

My brother knows more about cars than I ever will. But even he sometimes meets his match. He bought a 1950 Ford once that was in pretty rough shape. After working on it for many months, he felt overwhelmed and gave up on it. The car sat in the driveway for a long time, its dull brown primer making it look like a candidate for the junkyard.

Do you ever feel as though your once-bright hopes will never come true? Has your optimism ground to a halt? Do you no longer believe that anything good is coming in your future?

I've got some good news for you. God lives in your future. He likes you a lot, and He loves to get involved in making things happen for people He cares about.

God isn't just an observer, merely watching as your hopes and dreams wither. He cares about you. He created you for a purpose, rescued you at the cost of His Son's life, and wants to spend eternity enjoying life with you. He gets no thrill from your misery. God says in Jeremiah 29:11, **"I know the plans I have for you . . . plans for welfare and not for evil, to give you a future and a hope."**

There is hope in His Word. Let Him talk to you today.

Spiritual Denial

Children love to pretend. They have rich fantasy lives and effortlessly slide into their own parallel universes. Of course, the plan is that by the time they're adults, they can quit pretending and learn to see and accept reality.

If only. I bet you know plenty of adults who are still pretending. Single people move in with each other and pretend to be married. Married people act as though they are single. Sedated by drugs or alcohol, people pretend that their lives are fine. People pretend to be financially successful, but behind the scenes, they stagger under enormous mortgages, home equity loans, and maxed-out credit cards.

The worst kind of self-delusion is to pretend that you are morally good enough for God. You can blame other people for your sins. You can compare yourself with people farther down the food chain and feel superior. You can indulge in selective memory, remembering only what makes you look good.

God's view? Living in a state of spiritual denial is deadly. **"If we say we have no sin, we deceive ourselves, and the truth is not in us"** (1 John 1:8). You need help. I need help. God's help. And He will provide that help: **"If we confess our sins, He is faithful and just to forgive us our sins and to cleanse us from all unrighteousness"** (verse 9).

Self-control Is a Fruit of the Spirit

Not long ago, a soft-drink manufacturer got a lot of mileage out of the slogan "Obey your thirst." In other words, there is no point in resisting your appetites and desires. Go for it! The problem is that human beings have a lot of appetites—for food, power, excitement, sex, domination, money, and so on. The Bible tells us, however, that if we obey our appetites, we will become slaves to our appetites.

That's why it's so exciting to hear from the Bible in Galatians 5:22–23 that self-control is a fruit of the Spirit: **"The fruit of the Spirit is love, joy, peace, patience, kindness, goodness, faithfulness, gentleness, self-control."**

In other words, God not only warns us about the danger of living an out-of-control life, He actually helps us control our thirsts and all our other appetites as well when He offers us the living water that is Christ Jesus. Let the Spirit lead you today!

God Gets the Last Word

One of the girls in my sixth-grade class loved to see naughty boys get caught by the teacher. "Cheaters never prosper," she would cackle.

Ah, if only she were right. Alas, my sad life experience is that cheaters seem to do very well. Everything's a hustle. Everything's for sale. Them that's got shall get.

Do you ever feel as though you are wasting your time trying to get ahead through honesty and hard work? Do you ever fantasize about taking shortcuts to prosperity like everyone else? King David knew that feeling. In Psalm 12:1–2, he wrote, **"Save, O LORD, for the godly one is gone; for the faithful have vanished. . . . Everyone utters lies to his neighbor."**

But the planet is not out of God's control, and your life isn't either. He sees everything going on around you, cares about you, and acts at just the right time. That same psalm says, **"'Because the poor are plundered, because the needy groan, I will now arise,' says the LORD; 'I will place him in the safety for which he longs'"** (verse 5).

God always gets the last word, and His last word is "I love you. You are Mine."

God Is Steady

One of the most miserable features of life on earth is the puzzle of divorce. How is it possible that two people could become such bitter antagonists when once they were gaga in love? The sad reality is that not only do people change, but they can morph into personalities drastically different from the way they used to be.

A great gift to you from the true God is that He is as steady as a rock. James says that **"[He] does not change like shifting shadows"** (James 1:17 NIV). What this means is that His love for you is not based on your performance, but on an unshakable decision He made in His divine mind from all eternity.

When you are looking for meaning in events all around you, when you are tempted from painful events in your life to conclude that God is absent or powerless or aloof or condemning, just remember that His steadfast purpose for you will never waver. He will never stop loving you. And He will *never* tire of showing you mercy and forgiveness.

February 9

Live Humbly

Everybody knows stories about arrogant athletes or movie stars—spoiled, overpaid, hyped-up, and insufferable. You probably also know people personally who seem to think that the world owes them a living and that they are better than the "little people" around them.

But you may know also of athletes who appear humble and grateful on TV. They are quick to praise their teammates, respectful of their opponents, active in their communities, and they volunteer to work with disabled children. Don't those stories thrill your heart?

Sometimes God lets us experience pain and rejection as humility therapy for our own proud hearts. **"Clothe yourselves, all of you, with humility toward one another, for 'God opposes the proud but gives grace to the humble'"** (1 Peter 5:5). Isn't it funny? The more I make myself small, the more God lifts me up through His Word and Sacraments. The more I praise others, the more God praises me. Live humbly! And because this will be so beautiful and rare in our selfish world, you will shine like a star.

Connected to Christ

When we see people making fools of themselves in public or doing something embarrassing or illegal, our first response is to dissociate ourselves. "I'm not with *them!*"

One of the most wonderful things that Jesus Christ, our Savior, does for us is to choose to be identified with us. Not only did He take on human flesh just like ours and then stay human, but He takes particular delight in bonding Himself to us and us to Him, soul and *body.*

In the Sacrament of the Lord's Supper, Christ forms a communion (participation) with the bread and wine, and then when we eat and drink the Feast, He forms a communion with us.

"The cup of blessing that we bless, is it not a participation in the blood of Christ? The bread that we break, is it not a participation in the body of Christ?" (1 Corinthians 10:16).

What an honor! Every time you receive the Sacrament, you have a personal, physical encounter with the Son of God, who tells you all over again that He loves you and forgives you. Every time you receive the Sacrament, you realize anew, "Jesus, You're not ashamed of me! You actually like being with me. I am one with You."

February 11

Satan Is a Dragon

Okay, so dragons don't really exist. Yet stories of them appear in the literature of many different peoples over many millennia, and their general characteristics are well known. They have enormous strength and scaly bodies; they breathe fire; and their heavy, spiked tails are weapons too. But still, they are mythical creatures. Does that make Satan mythical too?

No chance. The harsh reality of pain and death forces us to see that evil is real, and so is Satan. John was allowed to see Satan in all of his ugliness: **"Then the dragon became furious with the woman and went off to make war on the rest of her offspring, on those who keep the commandments of God and hold to the testimony of Jesus"** (Revelation 12:17). John says that the dragon is filled with fury because he knows that his time is short.

This marvelous chapter of the Bible assures us, though, that Jesus Christ, the Lamb of God, has slain the dragon. Through faith in Him, we become conquerors also, and we overcome the dragon by **"the blood of the Lamb and by the word of their testimony"** (verse 11). So where does that leave us? Respect the dragon? Yes. Fear the dragon? No.

Not Guilty!

Some of life's miseries are pretty obvious—a car that's rusty and broken down, arthritic hands, an empty checkbook. Far worse, though, are invisible miseries. One of those is guilt. The past is unchangeable, and your mind can replay over and over evil things you have thought, spoken, and done. Try as you might, you cannot get rid of that bag of guilt, and you drag it around behind you wherever you go.

But Jesus Christ lived your life for you and died your death for you. God has declared you no longer guilty, *and so you aren't anymore*! Paul wrote in Romans 8:1, **"There is therefore now no condemnation for those who are in Christ Jesus."**

That invisible promise changes your status with Him. It also changes your insides. God likes and accepts you. You can forgive yourself and like yourself again. What's more, you now have a reservoir of goodwill to be patient and forgiving with the other foolish sinners around you.

February 13

Do Not Worry

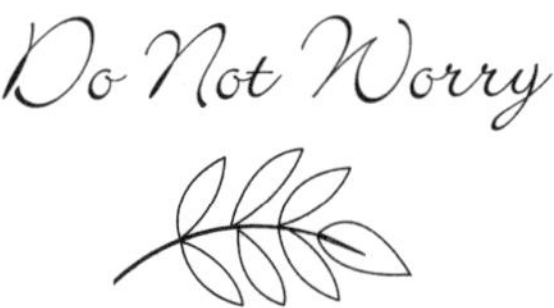

Are you a worrier? How can you tell whether what's on your mind is worry (bad) or just prudent concern and planning (good)?

Here are some diagnostic factors: Does your mind often panic? Do your thoughts generally jump right away to the worst possible outcome? Do you assume that bad things will happen and then lighten up only when the news is okay? Do you have very vivid memories of everything that went wrong in your past? Do you collect stories of friends' disasters?

Would you like some help, worriers of the world? Jesus said to His friends, **"Therefore I tell you, do not be anxious about your life"** (Matthew 6:25). If my next-door neighbor said that, I might just keep worrying. When my Lord Jesus says that and guarantees that His Father—who is also my Father—knows my needs and will provide at the right time, *then* I can chill. You can too.

February 14

Believe His Words

I wouldn't blame you if you didn't feel much like a star in your life. I wouldn't blame you if you feared that not only are you not a star, but you are throwing off so little spiritual light that you would barely qualify as a weak flashlight beam.

God sees that as no serious obstacle. In fact, He seems to do His best work with people who are broken and small or with those who are facing conflict and loss in their lives. After all, the power to change our attitudes and lives must come from Him first.

God chose two humble women living in the land of Israel to be the mothers of both the world's greatest prophet (John the Baptist) and the world's only Savior (Jesus Christ). **"[Elizabeth] exclaimed with a loud cry, 'Blessed are you [Mary] among women, and blessed is the fruit of your womb! . . . Blessed is she who believed that there would be a fulfillment of what was spoken to her from the Lord'"** (Luke 1:42, 45).

Never tell God what He cannot do. When He tells you that because of the work of Jesus in your life, you have great worth and a significant purpose in your life, don't argue. Believe Him. It's true.

What Motivates You?

Here's a Wall Street question for you: why do you think so many large companies have collapsed and filed for bankruptcy? All too often, it is the same old story of powerful people driven by greed—people who stole and lied on a grand scale. People had no patience for long-term growth, and they sacrificed everything to get stuff "right now."

What motivates you? What drives you? Did you know that the Holy Spirit lives in the hearts of believers and provides motivation to act for other people out of love rather than greed?

The Bible says in Romans 8:8, **"Those who are in the flesh cannot please God,"** and in verse 6, **"but to set the mind on the Spirit is life and peace."** In other words, believers in Christ have spiritual power within them to want the right things and to do the right things.

Not only will you be a lot happier when you let the Spirit lead. The people around you are going to love it too.

February 16

Seek First God's Kingdom

Ever play the "comparison" game? I'm flexible; he's wishy-washy. I'm principled; she's pig-headed. I'm a connoisseur of fine things; he's materialistic.

Are you materialistic? Of course not. Only other people are. But how can you tell if you're getting there? Here are some danger signs: if you generally measure people's worth by how much money they have; if you will sell out your ethics and cheat or steal to get what you want; if seeing other people's nice stuff makes you envy them and hate your own life; if acquiring stuff is your primary way of feeling good about yourself.

Will you let Jesus teach you a better attitude? He told His disciples, at least one of whom had serious money lust, **"One's life does not consist in the abundance of his possessions"** (Luke 12:15). What should it consist of? **"Seek [the Father's] kingdom, and these things will be added to you"** (verse 31).

Here is the number one materialism antivenin: making your relationship with God, through Jesus, the very first treasure and priority of your life.

Good Husbands Lead

These days, when guys' conversations turn to gender roles, the dominant mood is confusion. We don't know who we're supposed to be anymore. It appears that nobody expects or wants us to be Ward Cleaver. Now what? Do we still pick up the check in a restaurant? Are we still supposed to hold doors and always volunteer for the dirty and dangerous jobs?

Well, guess what? Healthy homes still do best when the man leads. When the man in a family is weak or absent, everybody suffers. True godly leadership is not about power or using others. Godly leadership is about going first in *serving* others. God calls His men not to be controllers or bosses, but *heads.* See the difference? Ephesians 5:23 says, **"The husband is the head of the wife even as Christ is the head of the church, His body, and is Himself its Savior."**

Heads who are like Christ accept responsibility. Heads who are like Christ take care of the other members of the body. Heads are wired to the nerve endings that send pain messages from all over, so when the body hurts, the head says, "Ow!" Kids, moms, you know the truth—life at home is awesome when Dad acts like Jesus.

I Am a Child of God!

When you first become aware of being a Christian, you have this rush of a sense of well-being. "I am victorious! I am invincible! I am a child of God!" And then the hard reality breaks in: suffering and hardships still bog down your life. Even Christians have their share of financial struggles, bitter family conflicts, and health breakdowns. Have you ever sighed, "Lord, why me?"

Alas, the world we live in is broken, and all people, Christians included, will have struggles. The Bible says in Acts 14:22, **"Through many tribulations we must enter the kingdom of God."**

Some of our hardships are caused by the cruelty or selfishness of others. Some are self-inflicted. And some seem to have no explanation at all.

When they come, don't panic. They are inevitable. But they are temporary. Like Jesus, we suffer on earth. Like Jesus, we will be glorified in our new home.

The Lord Will Lay Waste the Earth

Everyone in America has heard about what Hurricane Katrina did to the Gulf Coast. How suddenly those howling winds ripped the roofs right off houses! Even worse, when the levees were breached, how rapidly that rising water turned beautiful homes into mildewed and moldy trash. Possessions were buried under inches of mud or simply floated away.

How important it is not to fall in love with our stuff! A catastrophe is coming that will make Katrina seem small. Through His prophets, God has sent word that the earth as we know it will be utterly destroyed: **"Behold, the LORD will empty the earth and make it desolate, and He will twist its surface and scatter its inhabitants. . . . The earth shall be utterly empty and utterly plundered"** (Isaiah 24:1, 3).

Those who heeded the hurricane warnings saved their lives. Those who heed Isaiah's warnings and look to the One who has already saved them from their sins will save their souls, too, in Christ.

February 20

Jesus Christ Succeeded

How are you holding up? Are there some problems that are pressing down on you? Is anything in your life unraveling?

Look back to what started out as a horrible Friday, the day on which Jesus Christ was crucified. Satan was rejoicing at all the cruelty, injustice, suffering, hatred, and blood. But on the cross, Jesus Christ succeeded in paying off our spiritual debts, ending Satan's authority over us, and winning a "not guilty" verdict from the Judge of the world. Jesus entered the grave as a winner, not a loser, and three days later, He emerged alive again.

The prophet Isaiah was given insight into the true meaning of that mighty day: **"It was the will of the Lord to crush Him; He has put Him to grief; when His soul makes an offering for guilt, He shall see His offspring; He shall prolong His days. . . . By His knowledge shall the righteous one, My servant, make many to be accounted righteous"** (Isaiah 53:10–11).

When your days get overwhelming, look back to the Friday we call "Good" and find satisfaction in knowing that you are worth that much to God.

I Accept Responsibility

Are you a proud person? Is pride bad or good? You certainly been disgusted at some point by a braggart who was really full of himself. Have you ever been hurt by a woman who let you know that she was far above you? Have you ever caught yourself uttering arrogant words? We can all stand to work on humility in our words and tone.

But you know, there is a good kind of pride. It comes from knowing who we are because of Christ Jesus. Knowing Him motivates us to do our best and find satisfaction that comes from doing a job well, from learning how to take care of ourselves. Paul wrote, **"Let each one test his own work, and then his reason to boast will be in himself alone and not in his neighbor. For each will have to bear his own load"** (Galatians 6:4–5).

Parents, it's great that our kids need us, isn't it? It massages our insecurity. But it is far better for us to teach them to be independent and carry their own loads. Only weak leaders seek to do everything themselves. It's far better when people say "We did it ourselves" knowing that all we do is done to the glory of God.

FEBRUARY 22

God Is Omnipotent

How strong are you? How much of your world can you control? Can you bench-press five thousand pounds? Can you lift a mountain? Can you change the weather? Well, of course you can't.

But your God can. God is omnipotent. There is no limit to His power. When God came to earth in the person of Jesus Christ, His disciples watched in awe as He showed total mastery over all creation. The Gospel of Mark tells how Jesus' disciples were amazed when He silenced a violent storm that had threatened to swamp their boat. They asked, **"Who then is this, that even the wind and the sea obey Him?"** (Mark 4:41).

Isn't it good to know that wherever you sail your little boat today, the Master of wind and wave is riding along to see you to the other side?

The Secret to Contentment

Can I ask a personal question? How's your cash flow this week? I know that's a potentially painful question. The economy is not always perfectly robust, and some of you right now can't pay your bills. Some of you watched in shock as your retirement savings took huge hits because of stock market swings. Some "retired" people even have had to go back to work (if they can find it).

Money anxiety can make you miserable. But God is your best financial consultant. Paul said in Philippians 4:12–13, **"I have learned the secret of facing plenty and hunger, abundance and need. I can do all things through Him who strengthens me."**

Sometimes God tests us with money and sometimes with no money. But He always gives us enough. He has given us all we need—forgiveness, new life, and assurance of an eternal life with Him—not to mention all the other blessings of life. If we take the time to take inventory, we will discover that we've been blessed by the best.

Lighten Your Load

Why do you suppose so many people run away from God and try their best to avoid going to church? My guess is that a lot of people are afraid of getting hustled. They assume that the Church just wants to *take* from them. They assume that Christianity is basically a load of rules that will just add to their life's burdens.

Would it surprise you to know that God's basic message to you is what He wants to *give to* you, that God's first desire for you is to *lighten* your load rather than increase it? The Lord Jesus says in Matthew 11:28, **"Come to Me, all who labor and are heavy laden, and I will give you rest."**

Some possibly well-meaning religious people have tried to portray the Church as a country club, where membership brings exclusivity and insiders-only benefits. Some portray it as a gym, where you submit to discipline and work out until you look better.

In fact, God wants His Church to be a MASH unit out in the world, where medics can bring wounded people to be restored in Jesus, our Great Physician.

February 25

There Will Be Healing

Every winter, hordes of pale, half-frozen northerners flock to the South. One of their first rituals is to get rid of as much clothing as they can to allow that blessed sunshine to touch their skin again.

The prophet Malachi compared the presence of Jesus Christ to glorious sunshine. When He returns once and for all, everything will get better. **"But for you who fear My name, the sun of righteousness shall rise with healing in its wings"** (Malachi 4:2). These wings are poetic references to the sun's—Jesus'—rays.

May I say that I can't wait for that great day of healing? I long for the restoration of my body, and I long even more intensely for the healing of my soul and spirit. I will be glad in heaven that no one can hurt me anymore, but I am even gladder that I won't hurt anybody else. The blind will see, the mute will shout, and the disabled will dance. I will be well again, well in every way, and you will too.

February 26

God's Gift: Hardship

After a severe hurricane ravaged the Gulf Coast, I heard a radio commentator mock those who believed in "intelligent design." His point was this: How could an intelligent and supposedly compassionate God allow all this suffering? Why would God allow your heart or your health to be broken?

Hardship is not necessarily bad. Struggle can be God's gift. Paul wrote, **"I appeal to you, brothers, by our Lord Jesus Christ and by the love of the Spirit, to strive together with me in your prayers to God on my behalf"** (Romans 15:30). Paul had to wait. He had to work hard. He had to endure frustration, abuse, and broken plans. But all of those things made him a better missionary and communicator; they made him more believable and real to others who knew pain.

Great on paper, but hard to do, right? Do you actually want to join Paul in his struggle? Mental toughness does not come from vacation days. Jesus didn't say, "If anyone would come after Me, he should pick up his doughnuts and follow Me." Sometimes we need tears in our eyes to pray "I need You, Lord" and mean it. When all we have left is our faith in the one true God, then we realize that He is all we need.

February 27

Money and Values

One drug dealer says to another, "I know it's wrong, but the money makes it all right." You know, with a modest effort, you can justify almost any evil activity by the money and maybe also by the "good" things you will do with that money, like feeding your family or paying down your debts.

One of the great themes of literature is the ambitious man who sells his soul to the devil for short-term gain, like power, longer life, or wealth. Do you know the story of Dr. Faustus and Mephistopheles? Have you ever sold out your values for something selfish and stupid? Jesus said once, **"What does it profit a man to gain the whole world and forfeit his soul? For what can a man give in return for his soul?"** (Mark 8:36–37).

Time to take a values inventory. What are your three most precious possessions? What is the goal of your life? What does God think about how you are using His money?

Taking a values inventory of our lives might just lead us to see how much we need the forgiveness that Jesus offers to all.

February 28

Tell the Truth

Lies come naturally. Children do not have to take lying lessons or spend a week at summer lying camp to become skilled at it. They seem to discover distressingly soon in life that they can evade and shift blame, ditch responsibility, and avoid trouble by lying. It's so easy. It's just talk.

Adults lie just as much and more, although they grow more sophisticated and clever in their lies. Police crime investigations and courtroom trials would take one-fourth the time if people would just tell the truth—if they just wouldn't lie.

You are a child of the light, forgiven and changed because of Jesus' life and death; you no longer belong to the darkness. Be different. Here is a better way: **"Do not lie to one another, seeing that you have put off the old self with its practices"** (Colossians 3:9). Lies rot out your character and destroy it. Telling the truth, though it may bring short-term discomfort, hastens healing and builds character. God promises that your life will be better if you stop lying and tell the truth.

February 29

Subject to Temptation

One aspect of Jesus' saving love for me is that He doesn't despise me for being weak. He doesn't much like my sins, and He does hold me accountable, but He doesn't despise me. One of the reasons is that He had to wrestle with the devil too, and He knows how hard it is to choose and do what is right.

"We do not have a high priest who is unable to sympathize with our weaknesses, but one who in every respect has been tempted as we are, yet without sin" (Hebrews 4:15). Think of it—Jesus loved you enough to subject Himself to Satan's tempting, teasing lures. Think of it—He never caved in. His perfect track record against temptation made Him a perfect sacrifice on the cross.

Those terrible experiences of wrestling with Satan lead Him to be compassionate with us. **"Because He Himself has suffered when tempted, He is able to help those who are being tempted"** (Hebrews 2:18).

Where are you weak right now? With which satanic temptation do you need help today?

MARCH

The Lord will keep your going out and your coming in from this time forth and forevermore.

Psalm 121

March 1

Daily Bread

If you ever find work in a bakery, try to work in the retail end if you want normal hours. If you work as a baker, you are tending the ovens in the middle of the night so there will be fresh product at 6:00 a.m.

Your God has promised to provide material support for you and for your family. He doesn't drop it from the sky the way He sent manna to the Israelites. But He is up all night, baking your daily bread so it will be ready to go in the morning. Daily bread means that God is not aloof but actively engaged in your life, lining up the day-to-day resources He sees that you need.

When Jesus taught us how to pray, He invited us to appeal for daily bread not to a CEO or a dictator but to a Father. You can absolutely always trust in the kind and generous heart of the One who delights in calling you His child and has assumed responsibility for you.

"The reward for humility and fear of the Lord is riches and honor and life" (Proverbs 22:4). "Lord, I kneel before You and declare my dependence on Your providing. Lord, I trust Your wisdom, Your great strength, and Your rock-steady love for me. Lord, I will wait for Your daily bread, which I trust will arrive at just the right time. Thank You for all You do for me."

March 2

You Will Enjoy God's Praise

Children have an enormous appetite for words of approval. Saintly parents know that one of their main jobs is to praise and build up their children over and over. Maybe you know people who, even as grown-ups, feel that they don't have their parents' approval and that they have to beg for scraps of praise.

Get this—God recognizes and celebrates the things His partners on earth do to draw lost sinners to their loving Savior. If there is joy among the angels over one sinner who repents, how do you think the Father feels to get a child back?

When you use your gifts and opportunities in life to wake people up and show them what Jesus has done for them, God takes notes. And although this is not the main reason for sharing our faith, it's kind of exciting to know that our labors won't go unnoticed. **"Those who are wise shall shine like the brightness of the sky above, and those who turn many to righteousness, like the stars forever and ever"** (Daniel 12:3).

God's love and mercy motivate us to share Jesus with others. Hey—want to go to church with me this Sunday?

MARCH 3

No More Tears

Bath time for small children is partly fun and partly an ordeal. There are plenty of giggles with the bubbles, but there will be angry shrieks when soap gets in their eyes. Some lab and marketing geniuses developed a "no more tears" children's shampoo that takes the crying out of the experience.

Don't you wish you could shampoo your hair with some miracle substance in the morning that would guarantee that you wouldn't need to cry that day? The reality is that we have to live in a broken and sinful world. Stuff happens. We get hurt.

When you cry, God's heart aches too. His answer to your misery was to put His Son through hell on Calvary. That sacrifice opens up His pure and peaceful everlasting kingdom. I think we will like living there.

In Revelation 21:4, the Bible promises all believers that **"[God] will wipe away every tear from their eyes, and death shall be no more, neither shall there be mourning, nor crying, nor pain anymore, for the former things have passed away."** Really. No more tears.

March 4

I Am a Servant

I once saw a T-shirt in an airport shop that read, "Just do whatever I want and nobody gets hurt." Do you know anybody who acts like that? Do you act like that? It is a family's job to help each of its members find fulfillment in serving one another, not in taking from one another. But some strong-willed people train other family members to wait on them. Are you more of a manipulator or manipulatee?

Paul had a better idea. He wrote in Romans 12:10, **"Love one another with brotherly affection. Outdo one another in showing honor."** If our Lord Jesus said that He Himself came to serve and not to be served, how can we not want to be just like that?

Here is another of God's upside-down secrets to a happy life: Those who put themselves last will come first. Those who make other people feel important will themselves be praised. Those who cheerfully act like servants will be treated as heaven's nobility.

March 5

You're Not on Your Own

A repeated human tragedy that always hurts my heart is to hear about a child who was abandoned by both parents. The kid later says, "I've been on my own since I was ____," filling in the blank with some terribly young age.

Satan seeks to destroy you spiritually, and so he lies to you. He wants you to fear that you've been abandoned by your God, that you're on your own in life, that God only watches from above but is not actually engaged in making anything happen for you personally.

This is rot. God does indeed watch over you personally and individually, all the time. But He also acts on your behalf, giving you the things you need and arranging things to make your life better. Read Psalm 121 for its intensely personal comfort: **"The Lord is your keeper"** (verse 5). **"[He] will neither slumber nor sleep"** (verse 4). **"The Lord will keep you from all evil. . . . The Lord will keep your going out and your coming in from this time forth and forevermore"** (verses 7–8).

You never walk alone.

March 6

God Chose Kindness

You know, it takes absolutely no brains or character to seek revenge. Any idiot can brood over past slights and wrongs and dream about payback time. Jesus Christ didn't treat us like that. In spite of our acts of evil and rebellion against Him, He chose the cross; He chose *kindness* toward us. He didn't wait for us to clean ourselves up. He went first.

Now He invites you to treat other people the same way. The Bible says in Colossians 3:12, **"Put on then, as God's chosen ones, holy and beloved, . . . kindness."**

Being kind is making a conscious decision to choose to treat people better than they deserve. This is something you can try at home. How about it? Are you ready? Shock somebody today by the kind and caring words you say, even when the person doesn't deserve it.

You go first.

March 7

Wives, Respect Your Husbands

God commanded husbands to *love* their wives, which is a woman's greatest need. But He didn't tell wives to love their husbands. Not that that's unimportant—men like to be loved. But they absolutely *must* have respect. There can't be a healthy marriage when a man does not feel respected in his own home.

An episode of *Oprah* once featured a panel of married women who poured out stories about marital frustration. Whenever they got together with other women, the conversation was dominated by complaints about their husbands. Hmm. Is that your experience too? Women may have less physical strength than the average man, but their tongues can cut a man's self-respect to shreds and make him feel useless and small.

How's the emotional climate in your home? Could it be better? You might be surprised to find out that God has some ideas on this subject. He says, **"Let each one of you [husbands] love his wife as himself, *and let the wife see that she respects her husband*"** (Ephesians 5:33, italics added).

Now, dear ladies, on the assumption that God might actually be talking to you, how can you use your words today to build up the man in your life?

This isn't a burden for a Christian woman. It's a way to say thank you to Jesus for loving us and making us, the Church, His very own Bride.

March 8

Caring for Your Temple

Chemists and pharmacists have opened up new worlds in the human experience. Pills, powders, gel caps, and IV drips are available today that Paul and Silas could not have imagined. Some are legal; others are illegally synthesized. Some, when used under a doctor's order, can do amazing things to restore and sustain a person's well-being. Others deliver short-term excitement but miserable long-term damage to the human bodies God created and still claims.

As you care for your temple of the Holy Spirit, you will be tempted to take shortcuts to feeling good. Drugs, legal and illegal, are one of them. If a drug is illegal, that should settle it for a Christian. God calls us to obey all laws. But even legal drugs can be misused and result in physical damage and destructive addictions.

The real problem is a mind-set that values feeling good above doing right. Here is Paul's sad conclusion: **"Many . . . walk as enemies of the cross of Christ. Their end is destruction, their god is their belly, and they glory in their shame"** (Philippians 3:18–19). This is a false mind-set. The problem of sin is resolved only in the death and resurrection of our Lord.

As you make decisions about your own drug use, ask yourself these things: Is this good for my temple? Would my Creator and Redeemer approve? He lived and died for me. I now live for Him.

March 9

You Are Not Your Own

The magnificent victory that Christ won on His cross was not only for the purpose of liberating us from our worst nightmares—sin's guilt and power, the grave, damnation in hell. Christ Jesus set us free, but not to wander *on our own*. He set us free so He could then claim us *as His own*.

He desires nothing less than to remake us in His image: to think holy thoughts, love Him and other people, and find joy in being of service to His grand agenda. St. Paul wrote, **"Do you not know that your body is a temple of the Holy Spirit within you, whom you have from God? You are not your own, for you were bought with a price. So glorify God in your body"** (1 Corinthians 6:19–20).

The best advice that Christian parents can give their teenagers about going out on dates is to remember at all times who they are. They are not sovereign and independent agents. They are not their own. They are connected to a family. And they are loved and claimed by the Savior who died so that they could live.

March 10

Build Your Stamina

One of the most intense memories of my high school years was the season I ran on the cross country team. Every practice and every meet had my lungs bursting and my legs in agony.

Every practice and every meet was also a mind game. Why was I subjecting myself to this torture? Would I quit the team and this stupid sport? But as I learned to run through the pain, my body and my mind got stronger.

Paul knew that there is no gain without pain: **"We rejoice in our sufferings, knowing that suffering produces endurance, and endurance produces character, and character produces hope"** (Romans 5:3–4).

Doughnuts do not build a strong body, and easy money does not build determination. Learning how to live with pain toughens us. Life, after all, is not a sprint. It is a marathon. It is a race won not by blazing speed out of the gate but by endurance. And God wants so badly for us to meet Him at the finish line that He is willing to put us through some pretty intense conditioning to get us there with our faith intact. His Spirit runs with us, keeping us strong through the means of grace. Amen and amen!

God's Forgiveness Is Greater

Are you a *Star Wars* fan? Remember how Darth Vader fought off all of Luke Skywalker's attempts to bring him back to the good side? Vader thought he was too far gone. He had resigned himself to service to the evil emperor.

Perhaps you have felt that your sins are too great for God ever to love and accept you. Perhaps your years of guilt and shame keep you from God's house and from enjoying the fellowship of God's other children. Perhaps you are so aware of your unworthiness that you just can't bring yourself to pray.

The Bible says in Romans 5:20, **"Where sin increased, grace abounded all the more."** In other words, God's forgiveness is greater than your greatest sin. Christ is greater than Satan. God's mercy is greater than your guilt.

Perhaps you know someone who feels that he or she is too far gone and is resigned to fear and damnation. You can be God's agent of hope. Feel the love. Share the love.

Let Go and Let God

When you wake up in the middle of the night in a cold sweat, what is your worst personal fear? Come on, admit it. Everybody has fears. When you're little, it's the monsters lurking under your bed. When you're a teen, it's being rejected and having no friends. Young mothers worry about their babies. New homeowners worry about being swamped in debt. Later, your issues might be infertility, rebellious children, business failure, or an unfaithful spouse.

Whatever your fears may be, God is there for you when you need Him. He says in the Bible, **"Because he holds fast to Me in love, I will deliver him. . . . When he calls to Me, I will answer him; I will be with him in trouble"** (Psalm 91:14–15).

"Let go and let God" is a somewhat overworked cliché, but it's still true. Psalm 91 guarantees that the Supreme Power in the universe is interested in your struggles, cares about you in a personal way, and will get involved to help at just the right time.

I feel better already.

March 13

I Am Connected

Is yours a chatterbox family? When you get together, does the emotional level rocket upward? Do you all talk at the same time, interrupt one another, and just delight in what's going on in one another's lives? If so, you probably drive your in-laws crazy. But even if you aren't huge talkers, you have probably figured out by now that families need communication.

Talking to each other is oxygen for your family ties. Mom loves your calls. Dad appreciates the respect you show by consulting him. Grandma's loneliness is more bearable if she can hear your voice every now and then. And all those people even more intensely need you to *listen* to them. Their burdens are less heavy if they think that somebody cares about them.

We know that God cares for us. He tells us that He loves us over and over in His Word. We are always eager to listen to Him.

James figured out that the path to the heart leads through the ears, not the tongue. He wrote, **"Let every person be quick to hear, slow to speak"** (James 1:19). How are you doing? Hmm . . . tell me about it. I've got time.

March 14

It'll Be All Right

How are you feeling right now? How are your insides doing? Are you calm and peaceful, or are your feelings all churned up?

All of us live with a lot of stress. The people you pass on the street—yeah, the ones who look so normal—are dealing with debts, addictions, family breakups, job layoffs, health crises, STDs, and huge auto repair bills. But the worst kind of stress is living with a permanent fear that God is angry with us and is going to punish us sooner or later. But get this: one of the Spirit's main goals for your life, one of His *fruits*, is to give you peace inside.

The Bible says in Romans 5:1, **"Since we have been justified by faith, we have peace with God through our Lord Jesus Christ."** Whenever you let the Spirit speak to you through His Word, He gives you the calm assurance that you are God's child, that your sins have been forgiven, and that God actually likes you.

Everything will be all right.

March 15

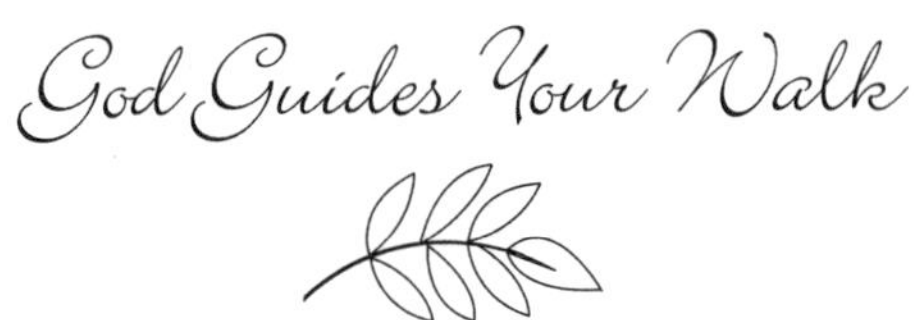

What do I do now?" Have you ever groaned that question? What could be worse than confusion? Sometimes our choices in life all seem bad, or they all seem dreadfully hard, or there are so many different choices. Do you stick with a difficult boyfriend? Do you rat out a friend who is doing something illegal?

Do you help a child do math problems, or do you make her figure them out on her own? Do you protect a co-worker, or do you tell the boss? What do you do about your daughter's problem pregnancy? How can you cope with bankruptcy?

Well, guess what? God guides your walk. He cares enough about your life to provide information for life's toughest questions. Do you feel surrounded by darkness and unsure of what to do? Let the light of Christ shine in. Let Him speak to you through His Word.

The Bible says in Psalm 119:105, **"[Lord,] Your word is a lamp to my feet and a light to my path."** There you will find the way to eternal life as well as true principles about how to think about money, love, sex, your job, your family, and yourself.

God Gives Spiritual Strength

Imagine the terror of sailors who are facing shipwreck. Imagine their great relief to climb into a lifeboat. But now there comes another ordeal: surviving in an open boat on the high seas.

We will never be able to say thank You enough to Jesus Christ for rescuing us from damnation. But it is even better than that; He not only saved us from our own shipwreck and condemnation, but He promises to help us each day with spiritual strength to keep going, you might say, in our open rowboats on the high seas of life.

Here is a Scripture passage that you need to keep in your mind always. God promises you in Philippians 4:13 that **"[you] can do all things through Him who strengthens [you]."** What that means is that you will receive power from God Himself to help you carry out His agenda. When you are tuned into God's plan for your life, you will find stamina, courage, clarity of mind, and words that you never thought you had.

Yes you can!

March 17

The Man of Lawlessness

When you need emergency medical attention, you don't have to worry about the competence of the doctors who attend you. In order to practice medicine, doctors need to pass and maintain rigorous state board standards. You have no such government guarantees for church leaders, though. And herein lies a sobering heads-up about your enemies: they have infiltrated congregations and church organizations too. Our enemies are not only on the outside, but Satan's sinister agents are sabotaging the Church's work from the inside as well.

Paul described this "insider corruption" as a "man of lawlessness." **"The coming of the lawless one is by the activity of Satan with all power and false signs and wonders, and with all wicked deception for those who are perishing"** (2 Thessalonians 2:9–10).

Don't be surprised by acts of immorality among church leaders. Expect that some theological professors will abandon the truth and teach lies from hell. Anticipate that some ecclesiastical authorities will abuse people with their leadership and power. Hold fast to your Bible, trust God's words completely, and hang on tight to the Savior that you find there. Then you will be safe.

March 18

God's Grace Is Free

Every day, you are reminded that there are some very wealthy people on this earth. You see their vehicles whiz by. You see the huge buildings they own. You don't seem to have much by comparison.

Every day, people say and do things that make you feel worthless. Every day, somebody makes you feel like a loser. Perhaps you call yourself a loser.

God happens to think that you are precious. Do you want to know just how valuable you are to God? Look what it cost Him to bring you out of hell into heaven: God's Son, Jesus, needed to come to our world to suffer and die a horrible death on a cross.

The Bible says in 2 Corinthians 8:9, **"You know the grace of our Lord Jesus Christ, that though He was rich, yet for your sake He became poor, so that you by His poverty might become rich."**

God's grace to us is free—but it was a very expensive gift. Today would be a good day to thank Him.

My Ultimate Family Is in Heaven

Isn't it extraordinary that God describes Himself in family terms, as a Father and a Son? Or maybe it's the other way around—that God's wonderful design for our lives is derived from His own holy identity. Isn't it extraordinary that the Savior came into our world just as we did—born wet, naked, defenseless, scared, and hungry—and that His first needs were met by a mother and stepfather?

Our first redeemed relationship with God is not as His employees or royal subjects or prisoners of war, but as His kids. The Bible promises this: **"In Christ Jesus you are all [children] of God, through faith"** (Galatians 3:26). Even if your earthly family has let you down, your heavenly Father will never stop loving you, claiming you, cleaning you up, and beaming approvingly on you. Your picture is on His fridge!

Nothing in all creation can separate us from the love of Jesus Christ, our Savior. See You soon, Jesus.

March 20

There Will Be Peace

Have you ever noticed how much of each day we face with an undercurrent of fear? Think how much time and energy is taken up by security thinking and planning. Think of the last time you crossed the street to avoid someone. Ever been in your car, noticed who was standing on the street, and quickly locked your doors? Do you put your purse in the trunk of your car to avoid a theft?

Even our computers need increasingly expensive and complex security software to protect our data from people who enjoy planting destructive worms and viruses.

Daily vigilance is necessary, but it is also exhausting. Your Savior wants you to know that in His new world, you will live in absolute safety. Everywhere. Always. Nobody is ever going to threaten or hurt you again. Isaiah says that even the animals will live in peace: **"The wolf and the lamb shall graze together; the lion shall eat straw like the ox. . . . They shall not hurt or destroy in all My holy mountain"** (Isaiah 65:25).

Everyone you meet in heaven will be your friend.

March 21

Heaven Is Our Goal

How many times do you think you have spoken the words of the Lord's Prayer? A hundred? A thousand? How many times have you said, "*Your* will be done on earth as in heaven"? Do you mean what you are praying? Did you realize that every time you say those words, you are asserting that God's agenda is more important than yours?

Some people find their trust in God draining away because He doesn't seem to be doing what they want when they want it. Think for just a moment about what God's greatest desire for you is. It is not to make you wealthy, famous, powerful, or even comfortable. It is to get you through the minefield of your earthly life, safely home to heaven.

Let God's ultimate goal for your life be your goal too. Replace confusion with this kind of clarity: **"We look not to the things that are seen but to the things that are unseen. For the things that are seen are transient, but the things that are unseen are eternal"** (2 Corinthians 4:18).

Ah—I can see clearly now. Can you?

March 22

A Quiet and Gentle Spirit

It's tough to be a guy, to learn society's rules and expectations and achieve respect. It is even harder to be a woman. Our society is merciless with its beauty demands. Every female, already vulnerable to insecurity and self-doubt, is tormented by heavy daily doses of advertising—images of women with perfect skin, nails, and hair; no wrinkles or sags; and perfect figures.

Women are told relentlessly that their worth is bound up in their appearance. Of course, since most women cannot possibly match up to the magazine models, thousands of cosmetic products (and surgeries) are available to help (and make money for the providers).

God has a different vision. It's not that He wants His female temples to be sloppy or unkempt. Here are His words to help you find balance. **"Do not let your adorning be external—the braiding of hair and the putting on of gold jewelry, or the clothing you wear—but let your adorning be the hidden person of the heart with the imperishable beauty of a gentle and quiet spirit, which in God's sight is very precious"** (1 Peter 3:3–4).

Will you accept God's opinion of female beauty? Men, will you prize and praise the beauty of a quiet and gentle spirit in the women in your life? Women, will you cultivate a godly attitude as carefully as you apply your mascara? Will you show others the beauty of a life lived out of thanks for the precious gift of Christ?

MARCH 23

We Will All Enjoy Glorified Bodies

I've occasionally heard people say, "I don't need money, fancy vacations, fame, or a huge home as long as I have my health." Well, what if you don't have your health anymore? Are you afraid of the aging process? Do you feel sick or weak or old right now?

If you're a believer in Christ, you can enjoy the wisdom and serenity that come with age, knowing that shaky hands and bad knees are only temporary. Soon we will all enjoy glorified bodies. The Bible says, **"Strengthen the weak hands, and make firm the feeble knees. Say to those who have an anxious heart, . . . 'Your God will come . . . and save you'"** (Isaiah 53:3–4).

Complete physical restoration of bone, tissue, cartilage, blood, hair, and skin is a piece of cake to the Lord of the universe. We're going to look so good in heaven that we will probably need name tags to recognize one another.

March 24

God Always Sends Relief

Have you ever felt totally exhausted—emotionally, physically, financially, spiritually spent? I don't mean "tired" in the sense of "I'm tired of spinach" or "I'm tired of that TV show." I mean drained—up all night with a sick child and then at work all day. I mean unable to sleep for days because of major postoperative pain. I mean drained by the daily struggle to raise a rebellious teenager. I mean bone weary from living in the constant pain of fibromyalgia.

God sees our needs, and after the long night of struggle, He always sends relief, and He's always on time.

I didn't make that up. The apostle Paul made a huge commitment to you on behalf of God. He wrote in 2 Corinthians 9:8, **"God is able to make all grace abound to you, so that having all sufficiency in all things at all times, you may abound in every good work."** Did you get that? Your God loves you so much that He will see to it that you have everything you really need to complete your life's mission.

March 25

You Can Feel Secure

What is your security blanket? Do the jewels in your safe make you feel safe? Does having loaded weapons in your home make you feel protected? Is your job secure? Are your friends loyal?

All those things can let you down. Your God will never ever let you down. Sit down, close your eyes, and rehearse in your heart and memory all the things in God's wonderful plan. When you recall all the great things He's done for you, when you go over all the promises He has made, then you will know you are safe. Your Father is a great big God, holy and perfect, faithful and true, steady as a rock. And He loves you more than a mother.

"I have calmed and quieted my soul, like a weaned child with its mother; like a weaned child is my soul within me. O Israel, hope in the Lord from this time forth and forevermore" (Psalm 131:2–3).

This is why we feel safe. This is why we feel secure.

March 26

We Will Be Like Jesus

Have you ever noticed that your praying tapers off when you have a guilty conscience? Guilt makes us slink away from God's presence instead of running to meet Him.

One of the greatest things about life in heaven someday is that we will be pure and sinless forever. Never again will we hurt or disappoint our heavenly Father. Never again will we feel shame and guilt.

The Bible says in 1 John 3:2, **"What we will be has not yet appeared; but we know that when [Jesus] appears we shall be like Him, because we shall see Him as He is."** You know what? I can't wait to be like Jesus. I am thrilled that my physical body will be restored from all its damage and imperfections. I am even more excited that my heart and soul and mind will be as pure as Jesus' also.

In heaven I will never hurt anybody again. In heaven I will never hurt my God again.

March 27

Teach Your Children

Why is it so hard to teach children to serve? Why is it so devilishly hard to get kids to think of other people before they talk and act? My eagerness to criticize my own children is tempered by some fuzzy memories of scoldings I got from my own father about my own youthful selfishness.

Raising children to have a servant spirit is terribly hard. But it is work that must be done. God provides both guidance and power in His wonderful Word. **"He [an overseer in the Church] must manage his own family well and see that his children obey him with proper respect"** (1 Timothy 3:4 NIV).

Parents, God has shown patience and love beyond measure in His big plan of salvation for us. He wants us to teach that to our children, to pass it on. If your children don't learn to respect you, they will probably not respect their teachers. Or the lunch lady. Or the crossing guard. Or their boss at work. Or speed limits. Or any laws. Or the police.

Or God.

March 28

God's Free Forgiveness

Hey—tell me the truth—could you use a little help in making your home life better? Or maybe you know someone whose home isn't very happy. How can you break out of bad emotional ruts?

One of the things that drags people down is guilt. When you're feeling bad about yourself, it doesn't make you humble; it just makes you crabby and abusive. That's why the Bible's message of God's free forgiveness in Jesus Christ is such great news.

Colossians 3:12 brings a liberating message to all believers in Christ: **"As God's chosen ones, [you are] holy and beloved."** You are holy, the Bible says, because you belong to God. And as you feel better about yourself because of that, you will be able to celebrate the good in other people. As you learn to see yourself as God does, as someone valuable and cherished, *beloved,* perfect in Christ, you can provide words of healing to the fools and sinners around you, who are just as broken and miserable as you were without Christ.

Who needs kind words from you today?

March 29

Help People

As you get older, you will probably notice more and more how God sends help to you through other people—their words of encouragement, their critiques, their gifts. Did it ever occur to you that you might be the answer to someone else's prayers?

God loves it when you share your toys. He loves it because you are helping someone He loves, and He loves it because it shows that you are willing to invest in His big agenda instead of exclusively in your little agenda.

"A generous man will prosper; he who refreshes others will himself be refreshed" (Proverbs 11:25 NIV). Did you notice the promise that God attached here? God never just takes from us. He never allows Himself to be outgiven. When we do His will with our money, He not only gives us a deep and lasting sense of satisfaction and a long-term joy without a hangover of guilt and depression. He also is perfectly capable of giving more right back to us so that we can do it again. After all, God has given us far more than we could ever dream of. Just think of the gift of His Son, our forgiveness, and our eternal life with Him.

We will be *refreshed.* That will happen. He promised, and He never lies.

March 30

God's Universal Mercy

Are you ever troubled by the fact that there's so much suffering in the world? Why does there have to be so much pain in our lives? The Bible tells us that the root cause of all suffering in the world is the miserable rebellion of the human race against a holy God. Adam and Eve started it. We continue it, and we are all suffering the consequences.

That's bad news. But the good news is that not only is there universal sin and universal judgment, but there is also God's universal mercy for all people, through His Son, Jesus.

In Romans 6:23, the Bible says, **"The wages of sin is death, but the free gift of God is eternal life in Christ Jesus our Lord."** No matter how hard your life is now, you have the promise of a perfect eternal life through Jesus.

Can you grasp the impact of the word *universal*? It means that you qualify.

March 31

Living Sacrifices

In the Old Testament, believers would bring animals to the tabernacle, ritually slaughter them, and offer the carcasses as sacrifices to God. This pointed to the ultimate sacrifice that would pay for the sins of all people. The New Testament tells us that Christ Jesus was that ultimate sacrifice. He lived, died, and rose to forgive us and earn us heaven.

Today God calls on you to offer a sacrifice, not of bloody animals and surely not for sin. That was done once for all on the cross of Calvary. You are to be living sacrifices. God has given you spiritual gifts, and He promises that you will find your greatest satisfaction in life as you use those gifts to serve people.

Not only has Christ forgiven you, but He has empowered you to be transformed in the way you look at your life. The Bible says in Romans 12:2, **"By testing you may discern what is the will of God, what is good and acceptable and perfect."**

And here is one of God's delightful paradoxes—the more you give yourself up to God as a living sacrifice, the freer you become.

April

For as high as the heavens are above the earth, so great is His steadfast love toward those who fear Him.

Psalm 103:11

April 1

Our Offenses Are Many

In family pictures from my childhood, you can count five children. But my mother frequently suspected that there was a sixth. His name was NotMe. NotMe was the child who smeared up the bathroom mirror, left toys all over the floor, and melted a plastic soldier on the stove. NotMe dropped chewing gum on the rug and broke the basement window.

The very first response of men and women who sin against God is denial. Not me! The Old Testament has many stories of the progressive spiritual deterioration of the people of Israel, and like you and me, they stubbornly denied at first that they had a problem.

The prophet Isaiah helped them to see that the economic and military ruin that was coming upon them was a direct result of their acts of rebellion. **"Our transgressions are multiplied before You, and our sins testify against us; for our transgressions are with us, and we know our iniquities"** (Isaiah 59:12). True self-awareness leads to sorrow. Godly sorrow leads to repentance. Repentance leads to faith in the one Savior who alone can bring us back to God.

April 2

Respect Your Parents

What is your motivation for obeying state laws and local ordinances? If you're like most people, you obey laws so as not to get punished. We all have enough grief in our lives; we don't need fines, driver's license points, jail time, or criminal records.

Is that your motivation for keeping God's commandments? Not when the Gospel of Jesus' love has touched your heart and won it over. When God's Spirit lives in your heart, changes happen. The more we are driven by God's forgiving grace, the more we can perceive the loving intent behind His commandments.

Take the Fourth Commandment, for instance. Prizing and respecting our parents makes their lives better, honors the God who gave them to us, and also carries God's serious promises to increase *both the quantity and quality* of our lives.

"'Honor your father and mother' (this is the first commandment with a promise), 'that it may go well with you and that you may live long in the land'" (Ephesians 6:2–3).

How can you honor your parents today?

APRIL 3

God's Love During Times of Stress

Have you ever noticed how stress can erode relationships? Marriages, for example, sometimes fray and even break up under the pressure of having to care for a profoundly disabled child or during a prolonged financial drought or military separation. Personal stress can also erode a believer's confidence in God's love. "I thought He loved me. Maybe not; is this a punishment for my past misdeeds?"

But here's one thing you don't ever have to doubt: your hardships are not punishments. God has already done all the punishing He needs to do, and it was done on the back of His Son, Jesus, on the cross of Calvary. God's forgiveness is not like ours. When He forgives, it is total, unconditional, and permanent.

Don't take my word for it. Here's God's: **"He does not deal with us according to our sins, nor repay us according to our iniquities. For as high as the heavens are above the earth, so great is His steadfast love toward those who fear Him"** (Psalm 103:10–11).

That means that in your times of stress, not only is He not angry with you, but He is planning the sweet things He is going to do to bring you some relief!

April 4

God Is Nice

In my favorite *Dennis the Menace* comic strip, Dennis is walking away from the Wilsons' house with his mouth full of chocolate chip cookies. His little friend Margaret is telling him, "Dennis, Mrs. Wilson didn't give you those cookies because *you're* nice. She gave them to you because *she's* nice."

Ever wonder why God likes you? There is something the Bible wants you to know about God. Romans 4:5 says, **"To the one who does not work but believes in Him who justifies the ungodly, his faith is counted as righteousness."** Did you catch that? God's grace to you and me is undeserved. There is nothing you or I can do to earn it. He gives us forgiveness just because He chooses to like us.

Can you see how this changes everything in your relationship with God? You don't have to endlessly justify yourself. You don't have to live in fear that you might not have done enough to qualify for heaven. You don't have to torment yourself because of past failures.

He gives you cookies because He's nice.

April 5

He Listens to You

You've heard stories about how shipwreck survivors, marooned on deserted islands, put desperate messages into bottles and throw them back into the surf. Talk about long shots! For all they knew, those messages were never going to connect with anybody.

Some of us are fearful or cynical and view prayer in the same way—as a forlorn exercise in communication futility. "Nobody's listening, and nobody's coming to help" sums up our pessimism.

Not so fast. The God who created us and redeemed us is also interested in helping us. Here is His promise: **"This is the confidence that we have toward [God], that if we ask anything according to His will He hears us"** (1 John 5:14). His listening ears can track any human attempt to communicate with Him—whether singing, whispering, shouting, or even thinking. Got that? The King wants to know what's on your mind, and His lines are open 24/7.

How about talking with Him right now? What would you like Him to know?

April 6

Satan Is a Liar

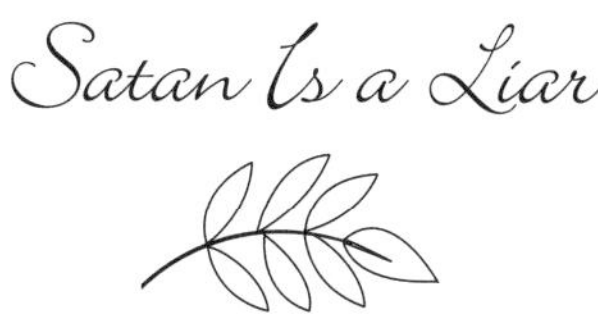

Don't you just hate being lied to? I hate the feeling of being manipulated, that someone is setting me up, making me out to be a fool.

You know, the king of liars is Satan, the devil himself. His ultimate goal is to destroy you spiritually, to separate you from God, and to keep you enslaved in your sins. So he tells you lies about yourself and about God.

He tries to make the Ten Commandments into the Ten Suggestions. He lies. He told Adam, and he tells you, that sinners will not surely die. He lies. He tempts you into sin and then tells you you're pathetic and hopeless. He lies.

Jesus tells you the truth. He says that **"[the devil has] no truth in him. When he lies, he speaks out of his own character, for he is a liar and the father of lies"** (John 8:44). How can you ever know the truth? Listen to Jesus. He is the way, the truth, and the life—and His truth will set you free.

The Savior's Completed Work

On the face of it, it might seem as though Jesus Christ didn't finish His job and that Satan is winning. Our lives are hurt by cruelty, crime, and disease. Violence is everywhere. Marriages are collapsing. Children are abused by people they trusted. People and nations hate one another.

Jesus died. Again, that looks like defeat. But He rose again. His resurrection guarantees His complete, unconditional victory over sin, death, hell, and Satan.

One Sunday afternoon, John heard the voice of the risen and triumphant Savior: **"Fear not, I am the first and the last, and the living one. I died, and behold I am alive forevermore, and I have the keys of Death and Hades"** (Revelation 1:17–18).

Jesus Christ gives you the gift of certainty, of a job completed. Your sins have been forgiven, your grave is now just a bed for a short nap, and your name has already been lettered on the door of your heavenly home.

Godly Patience

You've probably noticed how shortsighted children are. "I want it now. Right now!" Thinking ahead is a learned behavior, a skill that needs to be taught. It is easy to live for right now. Drug and alcohol addictions and out-of-wedlock childbirths "happen" to people who just couldn't defer gratification to a later time.

God's ultimate gift to you is to let you live with Him forever in heaven. But that wonderful destination can seem so remote as not to exist. Future-thinking is an important skill that each of us needs to cultivate in his or her own heart. Paul wrote, **"Put on then, as God's chosen ones, holy and beloved, . . . patience"** (Colossians 3:12).

Waiting is not weakness. It comes from the serene confidence that God will keep all His promises, that our future is going to be way better than our past, and that God is managing all the events of our lives to get us to the finish line with our faith intact. Wait for the Lord; be strong and take heart and wait for the Lord!

April 9

Let Jesus Carry Your Load

Blaming other people for your problems seems to work for a while. But eventually, the truth crashes in—your pain is self-inflicted. It's your fault. You cheated on her. You made the terrible investments. You took the drugs. You stole the money. You fired the weapon.

One of the most paralyzing of all human experiences is guilt. Guilt makes you think you're destined to be like that. Guilt smothers hope. Guilt just keeps digging the hole deeper. Guilt keeps you from praying or reading the Bible. Guilt makes you hide from God, the very one whose voice you most need to hear.

Jesus' mission on this earth was to neutralize and remove your guilt. His death and resurrection provide an unlimited source of the forgiving relief that we all need. King David wrote, **"When I kept silent, my bones wasted away through my groaning all day long. . . . I said, 'I will confess my transgressions to the Lord,' and You forgave the iniquity of my sin"** (Psalm 32:3, 5).

Ready for your load of guilt to be lightened? Throw it on Jesus today and let Him have it.

God Controls Nature

Sometimes the world we live in seems like a beautiful, peaceful place. But our environment can be nasty too—sometimes it seems as though nature itself is trying to destroy the people who live in it. Wildfires, hailstorms, typhoons, avalanches, hurricanes, tidal waves, and earthquakes can destroy property and people.

St. Paul explains why nature sometimes seems so broken. It's because it is: **"The creation was subjected to futility . . . in hope that the creation itself will be set free from its bondage to corruption and obtain the freedom of the glory of the children of God"** (Romans 8:20–21).

It comes as a great comfort to read in the Bible the stories of the miracles of Jesus and to watch Him work. Everyone who trembled as a child during severe thunderstorms will be comforted by hearing how Jesus could still a violent storm with just a word.

The Christian faith is not merely an interesting philosophy. It is trust and confidence in the One who made the world and who still controls it.

April 11

Pessimism

Are pessimists born that way or is it an attitude they choose? Your genes or upbringing may have contributed to a gloomy outlook, but God's Word will not let you stay that way.

You are not a slave to your attitudes. Your spirit has been reborn by the power of the Spirit. Your new Christlike self is in charge—you've been given authority and power over your crabby old self. Jesus has paid your debts. Satan is broken and doomed. Death is temporary. You have been preapproved for a suite in the heavenly mansions. So act like the winner you are!

You can choose what to let your mind dwell on. If you look for failure, ugliness, defeat, and pain, you can certainly find it. But here's a better way: **"Whatever is true, whatever is honorable, whatever is just, whatever is pure, whatever is lovely, whatever is commendable, if there is any excellence, if there is anything worthy of praise, think about these things"** (Philippians 4:8).

Both God's Word and God's world are full of beauty, grace, and hope. If you choose to look for them, you will find them all around you. Let your mind dwell on those things, and you will be transformed into an optimist.

April 12

The Brokenness of Self-hatred

Do you remember times when you have felt foolish? Do you like what you see in the mirror? Do you think of yourself as a winner? Do you like yourself?

Great numbers of people don't, and you may be one of them. Around twenty-nine thousand people commit suicide in America each year, and many millions more want to because they hate their lives so much.

How is it possible to be happy when you feel so bad? Step 1 is to stop looking inward, obsessed with your own feelings, and check in with God's opinion first. Here's where having a Savior in Jesus changes everything. Thanks to His perfect life, perfect death, and glorious resurrection, God has a new view of you. He thinks you're beautiful! He thinks you're worth claiming as His child and worth inviting to heaven.

In Isaiah 61:1–3, the Savior says, **"The Spirit of the Lord God . . . sent Me . . . to comfort all who mourn; . . . to give them a beautiful headdress instead of ashes, the oil of gladness instead of mourning."** You know, if God thinks you're beautiful, then you must be. If God likes you, then you can like yourself.

April 13

Balancing Work and Life

I don't know a lot of people who have found perfect balance in their work and family lives. Many times, I question my own time decisions. I know unemployed and underemployed people, and I struggle and grieve with them over their finances and feelings of low self-worth. I also know people whose jobs have consumed them, people who are hurting their families and draining their joy from life.

It is hard to get it right. Here's a little advice from Paul, a man who gave his all for Jesus Christ, but who didn't destroy himself or others in the process: **"Do nothing from rivalry or conceit"** (Philippians 2:3).

Here are some diagnostic questions if you fear you may be out of balance. Ask yourself, am I doing this just for money? Do I *need* this much income or just want it? Am I addicted to acquiring things or building up my own name and power? Am I hurting people? As I save and invest, do I also trust God to provide for me? Am I listening to my family's voices? Is there time in my week for reading the Word, worshiping, and doing service for the Church?

My answers to these questions might reveal a need to come to my Savior to ask for forgiveness for my imbalanced life—forgiveness that Jesus offers freely and fully.

Memo to self today: Ask key family member how I'm doing in balancing work and life.

God Changed the Rules

Everybody knows the basic rules of the legal system: acquit the innocent and convict the guilty. Convicting the innocent is called '"a miscarriage of justice," and acquitting the guilty is called "corruption."

You and I and every person on earth are hurtling toward a courtroom where we will have to give an account for all the years of our existence. The guilt you so often feel in your heart is a spiritual Geiger counter of the radiation of the sin that is there. By rights, you should be terrified of that coming encounter.

But Jesus Christ changed the rules. Paul wrote good news for you: **"[God] made Him to be sin who knew no sin, so that in Him we might become the righteousness of God"** (2 Corinthians 5:21). God wants you with Him in heaven so badly that He punished the Innocent One so that the guilty (that's you and me) could go free.

Your Enemy

Do you have enemies? I don't—at least I would like to think I don't. I try to live in peace with everybody.

But that pleasant little plan has one major flaw—the prince of darkness, Satan himself, hates me and you too. It is his prime goal to destroy me, body and soul, and he doesn't like you very much either. He hates God, and he hates God's children too. All of them.

The Bible says, **"We do not wrestle against flesh and blood, but against . . . the cosmic powers over this present darkness, against the spiritual forces of evil"** (Ephesians 6:12). That's the bad news. The good news is that God has not left us alone to fight Satan by ourselves. He gave His Son, Jesus Christ, to break Satan's terrible power once and for all by dying for us on a cross.

Jesus crushed Satan's power by allowing Himself to be killed. He gives you His victory. Through faith in Christ, you have conquered Satan too. Rebuke him and he will have to flee from you.

April 16

Share Your Burdens with Jesus

Have you ever gotten "the look"? After you've suffered a difficult blow, have you had people ask, "So, how are you?" You want to let all the frustration out, but you don't want to burden anyone. You don't want to whine and seem negative and obsessed with your problems, so you lie and say, "Fine."

You don't really expect any empathy from people who haven't shared your experience, do you? Do you find it hard to imagine that His Serene Majesty, the Most High God, omnipotent and timeless, could know what it's like to be in your shoes?

Actually, He does. Jesus, our Brother, does indeed know how you feel. Isaiah said of our suffering Savior, **"He was despised and rejected by men; a man of sorrows, and acquainted with grief"** (Isaiah 53:3). Have you found the relief and comfort that come from sharing your burdens with Jesus?

The emotional roller coaster of dealing with grief might make you want to isolate yourself. When you've been befriended by a fellow sufferer named Jesus, whose heart aches for you and with you, you will also have much more patience and empathy with the people around you. Jesus suffered everything we do—and more. And He offers the eternal solution to temporary suffering.

God's Children Overcome

By the time you are done with schooling and ready to enter the workforce, you may have all the excuses you will ever need to be a failure in life. Our world is full of adults who are haunted by past hurts and just don't think they can ever break free.

Paul had abundant excuses available to justify quitting his divine mission. He could have drowned in his own wretched, murderous guilt. He could have cited the physical abuse he suffered as a reason to play it safe and stay silent.

Instead, he learned to overcome. In Philippians 3:13–14, he wrote, **"Forgetting what lies behind and straining forward to what lies ahead, I press on toward the goal for the prize of the upward call of God in Christ Jesus."**

God's powerful presence in your life will be shown not only in the personal triumphs He gives you, but also in how His powerful presence in your life has helped you overcome your disabilities and failures. And more than that, He shows us how He overcame all disability, all failure, every excuse, when God the Son went to the cross for us.

Manage Your Anger

It takes no brains to lose your temper. It is so easy to go off on someone else, even someone you work with or live with, even someone you love. Angry words cut. They destroy love, destroy trust, destroy joy. Once out, they are like toothpaste—impossible to get back in. They live forever in people's memories and come back to haunt you over and over.

How do you find your temper again once you've lost it? Here are Paul's words of counsel for using your tongue: **"Be angry and do not sin; do not let the sun go down on your anger, and give no opportunity to the devil. . . . Let all bitterness and wrath and anger and clamor and slander be put away"** (Ephesians 4:26–27, 31).

You can't unspeak angry words. What you as a Christian *can* do is acknowledge responsibility for your previous temper outbursts, ask for forgiveness, and grow in the grace of tongue control. You can rebuke the selfishness in your own heart that thinks that the universe is all about *you*. You can grow in a Christlike servant's mind-set that uses ears a lot and uses the tongue to build up, not tear down.

Start right now. Who around you needs a word of kindness today?

April 19

Jesus Knows Our Pain

My grandfather used to say, "When you've got your nose in Limburger cheese, the whole world stinks." The point? Whatever intense emotion you are experiencing right now will color your entire worldview. If you are in pain right now, it can be very hard to be optimistic, to trust that your future will ever be better.

I used to think that old people moved around and walked in that slow, stiff, crooked way because they were losing coordination or eyesight. Chronic back trouble has helped me understand, as I myself have winced and limped through my daily routine. A great many people, old and young, are in physical pain all day, every day. That's why they walk that way. That also may be why they find it hard to trust.

Hours before His death and resurrection, Jesus predicted terrible hardships for His disciples: **"I have said these things to you, that in Me you may have peace. In the world you will have tribulation. But take heart; I have overcome the world"** (John 16:33).

Here is our hope—not in our tired and aging bodies, not in our brilliant minds or wealth, but in the words of the One who has suffered like us and for us and has conquered death, hell, and pain for us all.

April 20

It Is Finished!

Family members who have lost a loved one often remember with sadness the last time they talked with the deceased. Those "last words" stick in our minds, don't they? We hope that our last words will be weighty and significant, but they might just be trivial.

I will always remember a woman named Susan. As I visited her in the hospital, her telemetry sensors began to beep wildly. "Oh, shut that thing off," she groaned. Seconds later, she suffered another heart attack from which she did not recover.

As written in John 19:30, how different were Jesus' last words: **"It is finished."** With those mighty and weighty words, He announced that Satan was defeated, sin was forgiven, the Father's laws were obeyed, death's power was broken, and heaven's gates were opened to all believers.

Let Jesus' last words be the first words you go to in your time of need.

God Is Smiling at You

You can read a lot from people's faces, can't you? Without ever hearing a word, you can sense irritation, pleasure, doubt, worry, and fear. You can sense condemnation too. You can tell if someone is angry with you before a word is said. How good are you at forgiving people who have done you wrong? Not so hot? Do you hold grudges sometimes?

Sometimes we assume that that's how God looks at us—never really forgiving completely, still angry, still remembering our moral failures. If we try to imagine His face, we fear that He is frowning.

Our God eagerly desires a loving relationship with all of His lost and estranged children. That's why He arranged for our wrongs to be placed on the head of an innocent substitute, His own Son. That's why He instructed Moses to speak words of kindness to the believers and bless them like this: **"The Lord make His face to shine upon you and be gracious to you"** (Numbers 6:25).

Visualize God's face right now. Visualize Him smiling at you. He likes you, you know.

There Will Be Joy

I don't think I know anybody who doesn't get depressed occasionally. Some of my friends seem down more than up, and some friends need medication to keep them from falling completely into an emotional black hole. Many, many people feel bad a lot. Bad enough to shut down. Bad enough to avoid other people. Bad enough to drink too much and too often. Bad enough to hate themselves and their lives.

Here is a lift for the depressed: those who believe in Christ as their Savior have a beautiful and powerful promise from God that will make all our suffering on earth worthwhile. It makes me very happy just to think of how their first days in heaven will go, their first days without depression. The air will taste sweet, and they will want to sing again.

If you struggle too, listen to God's promise: **"I create new heavens and a new earth, and the former things shall not be remembered or come into mind. . . . I will . . . be glad in My people; no more shall be heard in it the sound of weeping and the cry of distress"** (Isaiah 65:17, 19).

Hang on, brother! It's only a little farther. Hang on, sister! You can do it. We're almost there. Don't give up!

April 23

You're in the Right Place

Did you become a Christian as an adult, or are you a lifer? What were your expectations once it dawned on you that you had been adopted by the Lord of the universe? Surely you expected that your life would get better and easier, and perhaps in some ways it did.

One of the nasty shocks of living the believer's life, though, is that in some ways, life gets harder. We discover that some of our former pleasures are actually evil. We might also encounter some abuse and hostility from non-Christians.

Maybe people don't invite you to social gatherings because of your faith. Maybe they mock you for being a narrow-minded fundamentalist. Maybe they roll their eyes when you talk about religious stuff. Maybe you've lost some friends. Let me tell you this—that's not a sign that you made a mistake in trusting Jesus. It actually means you're following "the plan." Shortly before He died, Jesus told His disciples, **"'A servant is not greater than his master.' If they persecuted Me, they will also persecute you"** (John 15:20).

Get it? If you are taking guff for your faith, it means that you're right where you're supposed to be.

April 24

He Became the Son of Man

Does the concept of God scare you? Does God seem remote to you—aloof, alien, totally unapproachable? In a sense, God has held Himself at a distance from His creation. Isaiah cried out to Him once, "Surely You are a God who hides Himself!" But the names He has chosen for Himself reveal a great deal about His identity and purposes.

Look, for instance, at the names Jesus gave Himself. His favorite term for Himself was "Son of Man." He could have called Himself "Glorious King" or "Supreme Dictator," but He chose to emphasize His human bond with you.

Think of it—the Savior took on human flesh to become our personal bridge to eternal life with God. **"The Son of Man came to seek and to save the lost"** (Luke 19:10). When He ascended to heaven, He kept His human body. And as a human, He will come back to give us the ultimate welcome.

He became the Son of Man so that we could be adopted as sons and daughters of God.

Our Greatest Treasure

Are you interested in being happy? Dumb question. Of course you want to be happy. One of the reasons why there are so many miserable people around us is that they are chasing things that don't satisfy. One of the most seductive, of course, is money. Many people believe that having more money will make them happier.

Here is God's way to a happy life. Are you interested? The Bible says, **"Do not lay up for yourselves treasures on earth . . . but lay up for yourselves treasures in heaven, where neither moth nor rust destroys and where thieves do not break in and steal"** (Matthew 6:19–20).

Money is a great thing. It is a powerful tool to make things happen, including making things happen on God's to-do list. But every last dime will be pried from your cold fingers when you die. The greatest treasure a human being can possess is the forgiveness and mercy of Jesus Christ.

You can take that to your trial on the great Day of Judgment.

April 26

True Brothers Care

Here are some easy things to do: judging others, criticizing, chopping down to size, staying aloof, not caring, running others down behind their backs. Here are some hard things to do: staying close to the family "black sheep," listening with an open mind, telling the truth in love, taking abuse.

Jesus spoke the following words originally about church brothers, but if they are true in church, how much more are they true in the family? **"If your brother sins against you, go and tell him his fault, between you and him alone. If he listens to you, you have gained your brother"** (Matthew 18:15).

I know, I know—guys love to compete. They are driven to compete. But guys, our true competition is not to outdo our brothers, but to develop our own God-given potential. If I am okay but my brother has fallen down, I will go back for him. God's goal for my role is not to win but to win him. Get it?

APRIL 27

The Mighty Nation of Faith

Have you ever been troubled by the suspicion that evil seems to be winning? Does it seem to you that Christian values are eroding steadily, that the number of believers is declining? Maybe you are a member of a congregation whose numbers have shrunk drastically over the years. You can see that militant Islam is on the rise again, even in Christian lands.

Are your hopes fading? When that happens, it's time to listen to a prophet speak, and who better than Isaiah? Here he comforts the remaining faithful believers in little Israel with a peek ahead at the tremendous success of God's rescue plans: **"Lift up your eyes all around, and see; they all gather together, they come to you; your sons shall come from afar, and your daughters shall be carried on the hip. Then you shall see and be radiant; your heart shall thrill and exult"** (Isaiah 60:4–5).

God won. His plan worked. You can be thrilled to be part of a mighty nation of faith and a winner in the victory over Satan.

April 28

Be Self-controlled

Are you impulsive? Do you come home from shopping trips with four times the amount of stuff you planned to buy? Do you plan to have one drink with friends and end up having three?

One of the reasons parenting is so exhausting is that children resist having to think, plan, and say no to themselves. It is so much easier to slide through life doing whatever comes naturally. "Naturally" usually involves leaving mounds of clothes lying around and homework undone.

Lots of grown-ups are really big children inside. It is easier to wait for other people to motivate us. Here is how a Christlike person thinks: **"The grace of God has appeared, . . . training us to renounce ungodliness and worldly passions, and to live self-controlled, upright, and godly lives in the present age"** (Titus 2:11–12).

Did you catch the key point? It is God's *grace.* The way we lead other people—and ourselves—to grow in self-control and personal discipline is not by making more rules. It is by absorbing God's unconditional love and by letting His power flow through us. It is by basking in God's high opinion of us and then living up to that honor. It is by letting go of past failures through Jesus' complete forgiveness. It is by believing that our efforts today matter and that tomorrow will be better still.

By grace.

APRIL 29

The Shield of Faith

So much of what we can *see* around us looks like defeat for God's people—Christians get injured, they get laid off from their jobs, they are victims of crime, they get sick, and they die. We all die—and this *looks* like defeat.

But the Bible says in Ephesians 6:16, **"Take up the shield of faith, with which you can extinguish all the flaming darts of the evil one."**

A shield is a defensive weapon. It deflects arrow, spear, and sword. Your faith is like a shield around your heart so that Satan's lies cannot kill your spirit. When he tries to beat you down into despair by showing you pain and suffering and defeat all around you, you can lift your shield and protect yourself.

Through faith in Christ, we trust that all setbacks are temporary and that every one of God's wonderful promises will come true for us—that He loves us dearly, that He is always near us to help, that He works all things out for our good, and that we have an eternal inheritance in heaven.

April 30

Our Spiritual Guide

What could be worse in life than to stumble around, confused and lost? Nobody ever plans to live like that. But you and I know plenty of people who are stuck in bad situations and just don't know what to do.

Jesus' disciples knew all about confusion. Even after years of personal example and instruction by Jesus, they misunderstood His mission and theirs, their courage melted, and they lived in fear. Jesus knew their weaknesses and had an answer. In the somber hours before His arrest and crucifixion, Jesus made a significant promise about a significant gift: **"When the Spirit of truth comes, He will guide you into all the truth"** (John 16:13).

The Holy Spirit, the Third Person of the Holy Trinity, is the creator and grower of faith and wisdom in people's hearts and minds. It was His power that transformed the disciples from cowards into champions, from confused fools to wise teachers.

If you are feeling confused right now about right and wrong, good choices and bad, let me invite you to pray to the Spirit to guide you as you read God's wonderful Word. You will get the wisdom you need. You will get the strength you need.

May

You are precious in My eyes,
and honored, and I love you.

Isaiah:43:3

May 1

Feeding Your Soul

We live in a restless age. People know that we are more than merely organic machines. People long for something spiritual, and they will sometimes adopt outrageous practices and beliefs to try to fill that aching hole in their lives.

In the severe day of testing that marked the beginning of His three-year ministry on earth, Jesus told Satan that man does not live by bread alone. People live by every word that comes out of God's mouth. Jesus told the woman at the well at Sychar that He had water for her to drink after which she would never be thirsty again. The writer of the longest psalm, which is a rhapsody on the delights of the Scriptures, worshiped his Lord: **"I will never forget Your precepts, for by them You have given me life"** (Psalm 119:93).

Nobody's life will be spiritually and emotionally healthy without God's Word in the center. Is morning, afternoon, or evening best for your quiet time with your Bible?

May 2

Prophesying

The school my youngest son attends has a program for "gifted and talented" children. Are you gifted and talented? Most people never qualify for a "gifted and talented" program or advanced-placement courses in school. You or people you know might be in that group. Yet, through your God-given faith, you have been filled with the Holy Spirit, and the Spirit has given you gifts.

That means you can consider yourself gifted and talented. The only questions that remain are identifying your gifts and deciding if you will use them in service to the Lord.

The Bible says, **"We have different gifts, according to the grace given us. If [someone's] gift is prophesying, let him use it in proportion to his faith"** (Romans 12:6 NIV).

To prophesy means to proclaim and explain God's Word. Are you good at that? Our world needs you, in whatever way you can, to help people see their own sin-sickness. They need you to help them see also the mercy and forgiveness of their Savior, Jesus.

May 3

You Aren't Worthless

Everybody I know struggles sometimes with the feeling of being worthless. That feeling is one of Satan's lies—he's trying to rob you of the comfort of knowing that God created you and the security of knowing that Christ rescued you.

Here's the truth of the matter: you are personally and individually valuable to God. Your rescue from sin and death was so expensive that it cost Christ His life.

God tells you, **"Fear not, for I have redeemed you; I have called you by name, you are Mine. . . . I am the Lord your God, . . . your Savior. . . .You are precious in My eyes, and honored, and I love you"** (Isaiah 43:1, 3–4).

When you listen to and believe these words, two wonderful things happen. First, you can start to like yourself again. Second, you will feel inspired to lift up the people around you and make them feel like they're worth something. God is pleased with both.

May 4

Joy Is a Gift

Blues singer B. B. King, with his beloved guitar "Lucille," once sang about the thrill being gone in his life. He was singing about a girlfriend. But there are a great many people who feel that the thrill is gone in their homes and in their spiritual lives with God. Is there more ill than thrill in your heart?

King David wrote, **"Restore to me the joy of Your salvation"** (Psalm 51:12). Can you see how this takes all the pressure off? Joy is a *gift* from the Holy Spirit. When we let the Spirit talk to us through the Word, He can go to work and change our insides, our thoughts and our feelings.

Through your Baptism, the Spirit has taken up residence inside you with all the power of the almighty God. He can help you focus on your treasures instead of the garbage in your life. He can transform your depression into optimism. He can change your sadness into joy. When the Spirit is in control, the thrill is back, baby.

May 5

Satan's Power Has Been Broken

Do you feel that you may be addicted to something? How can you tell? Addiction is any hurtful behavior that is compulsive, that you can't stop doing even if you want to. Addiction makes you a liar. You can become addicted to alcohol and drugs, the Internet, sex, eating, starving, gambling, working, and all kinds of other things. All these things replace the Lord as your God; that is, they become the central focus and organizing principle of your life.

Satan wants to keep you as a prisoner of your compulsive behaviors. Jesus Christ wants you to know that Satan's power over you has been broken. The Bible says in 1 John 4:4, **"Little children, you are from God and have overcome them, for He who is in you is greater than he who is in the world."**

It took the power of God Himself to convert you, to turn you from an unbeliever into a believer. Now that same power lives in you through the Spirit. Expect it. Call on it. Nourish it by reading and hearing the Word and receiving the Supper. Pray for it. Use it.

May 6

The Blessing of Parents

Yeah, I know. Not everybody has great parents. Some of you don't have any parents at all. As with God's distribution of other gifts, not everybody gets every gift. But there are plenty of good to great parents who get taken for granted, as though they were pieces of furniture or machines.

Were your parents okay? good? great? They are precious gifts of God to you, blessings to make your life better. Parents are God's stand-ins, providing security, food, guidance, and discipline. Parents help us fathom and navigate the complex ways of modern society. Proverbs 23:22 says, **"Listen to your father who gave you life, and do not despise your mother when she is old."**

The greatest parents are those who share their faith in Christ with their children. Did you learn about your Savior and His work in your life from a parent? You are blessed indeed. Are they still living? Perhaps you could call and thank them. Today would be a good day. Parents are good. God is great.

May 7

Contribute to Others

Do you think of yourself as a gifted person? One of the precious gifts God places in people is the spirit of generosity. The Bible says, **"We have different gifts, according to the grace given us. . . . If [someone's gift] is contributing to the needs of others, let him give generously"** (Romans 12:6, 8 NIV).

God's wonderful Word helps us see that all our possessions are loans from the ultimate owner. God's wonderful Spirit helps us find joy in sharing with and investing in other people. We have been given more than we need so we can have the honor and dignity of becoming part of God's team, working out God's loving agenda.

One of the mysteries of God's working is that although He could intervene in history and do one miracle after another, He seems vastly to prefer using people to help people. Think of all the people who have given you things. Imagine how useful you could be to God with a generous spirit.

Part of offering ourselves as a living sacrifice is to find joy in contributing to the needs of other people, rather than just in our own appetites and pleasures. Can't get no satisfaction in your life? Exercise your gift of generosity!

May 8

Be Content

Have you ever noticed how much of our life in Christ is a balancing act? God wants us to be self-confident and yet humble, self-reliant and yet dependent on Him, working and building for the long-term future and yet ready to die this evening.

God wants us to work hard, be ambitious, and not settle for second rate. But He also says this (through the apostle Paul): **"We brought nothing into the world, and we cannot take anything out of the world. But if we have food and clothing, with these we will be content"** (1 Timothy 6:7–8).

Is there a spirit of contentment in your heart? God's people take inventory of their lives and feel rich. God's people don't waste time comparing themselves with others or imagining that their lives are supposed to be trouble free. God's people pay attention to their blessings and count them—especially the blessing of a Savior from sin. God's people humbly expect only the basics in life and are surprised and grateful to receive so many treats.

I love my God who has blessed me with free forgiveness in Jesus. He continues to bless me day by day. Say it with me: "I love my life."

MAY 9

Dress for God

Clothes are part of our society's way to project beauty and femininity. They are also tools for projecting sexuality.

There is power in sex—power to get attention, favors, and money. Every new fashion season brings another wave of pressure to sexualize women more and to wear clothes that are tighter and skimpier. Young women figure out pretty quickly that projecting sexuality gets men's attention and money. What many women do not understand is that it does not get men's love and respect.

Nor does it get God's respect. He has a better way. **"Women should adorn themselves in respectable apparel, with modesty and self-control, not with braided hair and gold or pearls or costly attire, but with what is proper for women who profess godliness—with good works"** (1 Timothy 2:9–10).

What's in your closet? What will you put on the temple today? Christ's robe of righteousness, stitched on the cross of Calvary, will always make the perfect outfit.

May 10

Gentleness Is Strength

Middle school–age boys will tell you why they fight on the playground: "Because if you don't fight, people will think you're weak." I supposed some of us fight at home for that same reason—so our family members won't push us around or so we won't seem weak.

Actually, choosing to back away from violent speech and actions is not weakness but strength. The Bible says, **"As God's chosen people, holy and dearly loved, [put on] . . . gentleness"** (Colossians 3:12 NIV).

Jesus had every reason to fight back when His enemies wanted to kill Him. But He didn't. In agony from the cross, He gently asked His heavenly Father to forgive them, not retaliate against them.

Being intentionally gentle means that you return a soft word for a hard one, that you refuse to let a dig escalate into insults, and that you refuse to let insults escalate into a fight.

I think I know why you are afraid to do this. You fear that you will get walked over. You fear that people will take advantage of you. I know. Do it anyway. Care to give it a try? Gentleness is God's magic for a happy home.

May 11

Praying During Times of Loss

Doesn't it break your heart to see a child hurt? When your little child or grandchild runs into a table and smacks her mouth, how do you feel? Bored? Indifferent? Of course not! Your heart breaks, and you tend to the split lip and comfort her and soothe her.

Know what? God loves you even more than you love your children and grandchildren. When you run into trouble and smack your face, His big heart breaks too.

Jesus once told a story to His disciples to show them how much their Father cares for them and how they should never give up on praying: **"Will not God give justice to His elect, who cry to Him day and night? Will He delay long over them?"** (Luke 18:7). Every prayer gets instantaneous processing in the mind of God, and every request will be handled in the way that blesses you most, according to His great wisdom.

So why don't you use that privilege right now? I mean it. What do you need? Where does it hurt? Talk to your Father. He would absolutely love to hear from you.

May 12

God Makes Us Bigger People

We all know that suffering touches all people's lives, including Christian lives. We know that God allows us to be wounded and allows us to wound ourselves. But did you know that sometimes God *sends* hardships on you? Does that make you want to shout, "God, what kind of a Father are You, anyway?"

Actually, it makes Him a loving Father. Sometimes God makes us bigger people by taking things like money and health away from us. The Bible says in Hebrews 12:5–7, **"My son, do not regard lightly the discipline of the Lord, nor be weary when reproved by Him. For the Lord disciplines the one He loves. . . . It is for discipline that you have to endure. God is treating you as sons."**

Children may think math homework is torture, but the mental workout teaches valuable problem-solving and number-management skills. People learning a foreign language groan as they labor at memorizing new words, but the reward is enhanced communication skills. When your life is hard, let God use those times to increase and strengthen your faith in His power and promises. That will make you bigger.

May 13

Choose Your Friends Carefully

Most of the Christian life is a balancing act. We want to be concerned, yet optimistic; serious, yet joyful; sober, yet playful.

We want to be open to everyone but cautious in choosing friends. Almost nobody thinks about this when deciding whom to hang around with. But the truth is, you will start to think like and talk like the people with whom you associate. God says, **"Blessed is the man who walks not in the counsel of the wicked"** (Psalm 1:1). If you hang with sarcastic and critical people, your tongue will get sharper. If you hang with people whose language is full of profanity and cussing, your mouth will get fouler. If your friends don't go to church, you will more easily find excuses not to go.

But the reverse is true as well. If your friends pray, you will talk to God more often. If your friends use God's name in praise and blessing, your mouth will be holier. And get this: if you start to stray and exhibit danger signals, Christian friends will intervene to pull you back and remind you that you are forgiven for walking the wrong paths.

MAY 14

Your Living Redeemer

There are times in our lives when we feel strong, smart, invincible, immortal, and totally in control. And then there are those times when we know we are broken, miserable, weak, lost, and trapped. The apostle Paul didn't mind those times. God had told him, **"My grace is sufficient for you, for My power is made perfect in weakness"** (2 Corinthians 12:9).

That's why Paul could conclude, **"Therefore I will boast all the more gladly of my weaknesses, so that the power of Christ may rest upon me. For the sake of Christ, then, I am content with weaknesses, insults, hardships, persecutions, and calamities. For when I am weak, then I am strong"** (verses 9–10).

One of the most precious names for our God is *Redeemer*. A redeemer is a mighty rescuer—often a relative—who bails you out of a tough situation at great personal cost.

You have a living Redeemer in Jesus, who willingly gave His life so you could live with Him forever. He doesn't mind it at all when you feel weak. When you are full of yourself and proud, you don't feel like you need God. It is only when you cry out your need to Him that He can fill it with Himself.

May 15

Happiness through Respect

There's a sign hanging in a few of the kitchens that I've been in over the years; it reads, "If Mama ain't happy, ain't nobody happy." Well, how happy is Mama at your house?

Over the centuries, unhappy women have found many, many ways to change their husbands' behavior: from nagging to ridicule to a certain "coldness." And when the men don't turn out the way they envisioned, they can use their tongues to devastating effect and chop their husbands down to nothing. Of course, the men then withdraw their love and emotional support.

There's another way. The Bible says in Ephesians 5:33 that for a happy home, **"let the wife see that she respects her husband."** Men like to be loved, but we absolutely must have respect. It is oxygen for our soul. We don't always deserve it, but we wither without it.

Wives, would God lie to you? He is the God of unconditional love—love that none of us deserves. But through Christ, the heavenly Bridegroom, we have it! Try His way for a change.

May 16

You Are God's Prophets

Yes, you are prophets too. Not in the narrow sense of those specially chosen people who displayed miraculous abilities, directly revealed messages from God, and authored books of the Bible like Daniel and Ezekiel. But you are indeed a prophet in the wider sense of one who speaks God's words and carries God's power and authority.

Joel foretold the New Testament age that dawned when the Pentecost miracle occurred (see Acts 2). We are still riding the waves generated by that mighty outpouring of God's Holy Spirit, and one of the characteristics of this new age is that all Christians are priests of God and have personal prophetic ministries.

Here's your commission: **"It shall come to pass afterward, that I will pour out My Spirit on all flesh; your sons and your daughters shall prophesy, your old men shall dream dreams, and your young men shall see visions. Even on the male and female servants in those days I will pour out My Spirit"** (Joel 2:28–29).

Are you shocked at this honor? When people hear you tell Bible stories and pass on the warnings and promises from the Word, they are hearing the very voice of God.

May 17

I Can Feel Joy

Nervous, superstitious people can't ever allow themselves to bask in the pure joy of beautiful days. "We'll pay for this later." "Knock on wood," they mutter, looking over their shoulders.

You know, when the fear and guilt have been peeled off our lives, we can see God's kindness and blessings all over the place. Because we have a Savior, everything works together. Remember how the virgin mother couldn't contain her joy at hearing of God's plans? **"My soul magnifies the Lord, and my spirit rejoices in God my Savior"** (Luke 1:46–47).

Let your spirit rejoice too. Let Satan and his demons stew—drive 'em crazy and laugh at 'em. Tell them to be gone with their crabby, bitter resentments. This is a day that the Lord has made. We will rejoice and be *glad* in it!

May 18

Works in Progress

I love the words spoken years ago by a Christian senior citizen in the South. She said, "Well, I ain't what I oughta be, but praise God, I ain't what I was, and I ain't what I'm gonna be." This dear soul saw herself as a work in progress, and that's how God sees us too.

It's also how He'd like us to see one another. The people you live with are not finished products, ready to be judged. God isn't done with them yet. He deals with us patiently, giving us encouragement and time to grow, and that's the emotional climate He'd like to see in your home too.

St. Paul wrote, **"Work out your own salvation with fear and trembling, for it is God who works in you, both to will and to work for His good pleasure"** (Philippians 2:12–13).

You ain't what you could be, but praise God, you ain't what you were, and you ain't what you're gonna be.

May 19

Loving Discipline

Women love emotional sharing. Sometimes their husbands drive them crazy because they just don't seem to feel anything or want to talk about things of the heart. But, ladies, there is a huge upside here. Men can discipline without melting emotionally. They can insist on right behavior even when the kids think they are too cool, too busy, or too smart to have to endure this clearly unnecessary hardship.

Happy is the family in which there is a man who knows how to show tough love. God's view? **"For the moment all discipline seems painful rather than pleasant, but later it yields the peaceful fruit of righteousness to those who have been trained by it"** (Hebrews 12:11). God showed tough love when He forsook His own Son on the cross. It wasn't for His Son's benefit. It was for ours. It yielded perfect righteousness for us.

Because God made males less emotionally vulnerable, they can ignore the squawking and woofing that always erupts from immature youth and not take it personally or cave in. Isn't it a pleasure to be with children whose dad has spent the energy and time to discipline them when they were young? Paging all dads: your family needs your loving discipline!

Speak the Truth in Love

Okay, so I'm going to use my mouth today to build up, not tear down. But what if I see things that aren't right? What if a woman I know is flirting with a married man? What if my co-worker is stealing from the company? What if my friend is cheating on his wife?

God's people speak the truth in love—not to puff themselves up, not to feel superior, but to rescue precious human beings from paths of destruction. James wrote, **"My brothers, if anyone among you wanders from the truth and someone brings him back, let him know that whoever brings back a sinner from his wandering will save his soul from death and will cover a multitude of sins"** (James 5:19–20).

We are too often silent because we don't want to judge. We are all too aware of our own failings and don't want to be hypocrites. We don't want to risk a friendship or risk rejection.

Speak up anyway. As long as your words of correction are drawn from God's Word and come from a loving heart, they can only heal, not destroy. Speak up. If people are saved because of your example of faith and forgiveness, they will have an eternity in heaven to get over their irritation.

May 21

Your Children Are Not Alone

Are your kids on your mind a lot? Do you get panicky about them? Do you have nightmares about your toddler escaping out into the street? Or that one of your grade-schoolers will be abducted from a playground? Or that your teenagers will be the victims of violence?

Jesus wants you to know that your children are not helpless, and they are not alone. When your kids were baptized, God took on the obligations of a father. They now wear the uniform of His team, the robes of the holiness of His Son. He assigned special angels to keep watch over His little ones and protect them.

Jesus once said of little ones, **"I tell you that in heaven their angels always see the face of My Father who is in heaven"** (Matthew 18:10). Did you catch that? Children really do have guardian angels—it's not a myth. Angels have speed, intelligence, and great power, and they delight in serving the children of God.

Don't you feel better already?

May 22

The Brokenness of Feeling Doomed

"The apple doesn't fall far from the tree." Ever hear that saying? I think it means that we are all very much like our parents, that the way we were raised will strongly influence our future. That's a sweet thought if your parents were great role models. It is a terrifying thought if your home was violent, angry, dysfunctional, cold, or perfectionistic.

People talk all the time about destiny, about fate, as though their futures have already been written by some unknown and unknowable force. That's baloney. We are indeed influenced by our past, but we are not controlled by our past, nor by a mysterious destiny or fate.

Our Lord is much more interested in our future than in our past. He sends us His Spirit, who is greater than the sin within us. The Holy Spirit even prays for us when we don't know what to say: **"The Spirit helps us in our weakness. For we do not know what to pray for as we ought, but the Spirit Himself intercedes for us with groanings too deep for words"** (Romans 8:26).

What kind of person would you like to be? Let God help you chart your own course.

May 23

You Belong to God

Everybody has been bullied at one time or other. People assume that those doing the putting down must feel powerful, but actually it's the reverse. People who hurt other people really don't like themselves much, and so they want to drag others down to their own level of emotional misery.

We'd all have to admit that there are things about our own lives that we don't like, and so we don't like ourselves all that much either. The evil one wants us to think that we are worthless trash. He will use the meanness and cruelty of others, as well as our own weaknesses and failures, to make us loathe ourselves.

Here's why we need God so much. We depend on God's high opinion of us to give us a reason to believe not only in Him, but in ourselves again. Scripture says, **"God shows His love for us in that while we were still sinners, Christ died for us"** (Romans 5:8).

Imagine that! The Lord Jesus thinks you are so precious that He was willing to die for you in your messy state. He didn't wait for you to clean yourself up first. He died so you could *belong* to Him. If He thinks you're valuable, then you must be valuable. If He thinks you're worth dying for, then you must be precious indeed. If He sends His Holy Spirit to live within you, then you are not helpless. If He loves you, then you can love yourself again.

May 24

Rejoice in Your Singleness

Isn't it amazing how much of human life is structured around mating rituals? The "personal" columns in my local newspaper are loaded with "men seeking women" and "women seeking men" ads (plus many more types of seeking that ought not to be happening). Bars on weekends are full of people looking for love. Online networks and text messaging help lonely but cautious people who are looking for true love.

You have probably heard church talk extolling the merits of marital bliss. Does it surprise you to know that God thinks that being single is also a great way to live? One of the most famous bachelors of all time loved the independence his singleness brought him. Paul counseled, **"It is good for a man not to marry. . . . Those who marry will face many troubles in this life, and I want to spare you this"** (1 Corinthians 7:1, 28 NIV).

When Jesus gave up His life for people, He did it for the single and married, young and old. Our relationship with God doesn't depend on our marital status, only on Him. Who we are in this life is because of whom He called us and made us to be.

So before you curse your singleness, realize that marriage does not automatically turn an unhappy person into a happy person. If you are single, find the joy and blessings that your kind Father has placed there for you. If you are single, practice saying this: "I love my life."

May 25

I Owe My Family

It is not particularly hard to *sound* like a Christian. Talking the talk is not too tough—all it takes is some "Hallelujahs" and "Amens" and "Yes, Lords." *Looking* like an authentic Christian is harder, because when Jesus said, "Take up your cross and follow Me," He invested His whole life in His commitment.

We live in a country with so many social programs and entitlements that people look to the government first for their needs. Paul challenges us to live out our faith in our Savior in the way we show family loyalty and family support for relatives who struggle. He wrote, **"If anyone does not provide for his relatives, and especially for members of his household, he has denied the faith and is worse than an unbeliever"** (1 Timothy 5:8). Christian love shows itself in caring for others.

Do you know who are some of my greatest heroes? People who have sacrificed huge amounts of their own time, energy, and treasure to care for a child with Down syndrome, frail parents, or a foster kid when they could have easily pushed those people into an institution. God agrees with me. You rock!

May 26

Encourage Others

Are you a gifted person? Do you think of yourself as gifted? If your definition of "gifted" is restricted to being a world-class violinist or physicist, you might think, "No, I'm not gifted; I'm pretty ordinary."

God has a much broader view of gifts. Just as He brought you to faith in Jesus Christ, He also placed His gift-giving Spirit in you so that you could offer yourself as a living sacrifice back to Him. All of God's people have something to give. The Bible says, **"We have different gifts, according to the grace given us. . . . If [someone's gift] is encouraging, let him encourage"** (Romans 12:6, 8 NIV).

Think of it—God highly prizes those who have the ability to lift others up by their kind words and praise. I know how I vacuum up praise. Kind words are oxygen for my soul. What I forget is that God wants me to be even more interested in lifting up the bruised and wounded souls around me.

Who needs your encouragement today?

May 27

Open Your Eyes

It's hard to trust in God for the future if you think that your present life is a dry, parched desert. Satan works very hard on your head to convince you that you have nothing, that you are doomed to a life of disappointment and frustration. He massages your wounded ego to seduce you into thinking that you've been cheated in life, that nothing is working for you, now or ever.

That's not reality, though; it's just ignorance or worse—blindness to the wonderful things that God has been doing for His believers. Paul wrote to some Christians who were being tempted to think they had nothing: **"Blessed be the God and Father of our Lord Jesus Christ, who has blessed us in Christ with every spiritual blessing in the heavenly places, even as He chose us in Him before the foundation of the world"** (Ephesians 1:3–4).

As you put Jesus' Gospel glasses on, as you see yourself as loved and forgiven, you can start noticing the good things that have been there all along: faithful friends, dear family members, skills and gifts, daily bread, flowers and sunsets, and a faithful Savior, whose promise of everlasting life cannot be taken away from you.

May 28

True Brothers Help

"He ain't heavy; he's my brother." Okay, okay. That's a corny, overused cliché. But you know what? It's true!

Maybe you have a brother or sister who has made a string of bonehead decisions. He or she has used drugs, had children outside of marriage, squandered money, destroyed a marriage; maybe her or she can't seem to hold down a job. What are you supposed to do? It's not *your* job to take care of him or her, is it?

God says, **"Bear one another's burdens, and so fulfill the law of Christ"** (Galatians 6:2). This doesn't mean babying people or enabling destructive behavior. It does mean lifting them to the Lord in prayer. It does mean helping them connect or reconnect with God's mercy and His power and guidance. It does mean treating people with unconditional love and hope. It does mean taking some risks and cheerfully sharing your own resources when someone is down.

How would you like to be treated if your life had collapsed?

May 29

Here's a question for you today: how do you find God's actions—puzzling or clear? The answer is both of the above. There is, for example, no mistaking the clear intent of Jesus' healing miracles—He loves people and delights in ending their misery.

But sometimes God sends or allows things that seem destructive to us. Sometimes His pace seems slow, or He seems absent altogether. But nothing can change His steady love for His people.

In times of fear and doubt, Isaiah 55:8–9 reminds us, **"My thoughts are not your thoughts, neither are your ways My ways, declares the Lord. For as the heavens are higher than the earth, so are My ways higher than your ways and My thoughts than your thoughts."**

Someday everything will make sense. In the meantime, it is a comfort to realize that God doesn't expect us to understand everything He's up to. He just wants us to relax and trust His wisdom, power, and heart.

May 30

Teachers Are Instruments of God

I saw a bumper sticker a while ago that got me smiling. It read, "If you can read this, thank a teacher." It also got me thinking about how the ability to teach is a precious gift from God.

The Bible says we have different gifts according to the grace given us. If some people have the gift of teaching, let them teach. If you have the ability to convey knowledge, manage people, and communicate—and if you also have the stamina to put up with the whole process—that's a gift.

Asaph wrote that **"[God] appointed a law in Israel, which He commanded our fathers to teach to their children, that the next generation might know them, the children yet unborn, and arise and tell them to their children, so that they should set their hope in God"** (Psalm 78:5–7).

Training and discipling young people is exhausting work, but it's crucially important. All Christian behaviors are learned behaviors. Christian teachers are instruments of God in growing His kingdom here on earth. Let's find and encourage all of God's people who are gifted to teach, and let the children come to Him.

May 31

God Makes the Rules

What would you think of a football team that insisted its offense needed to gain only five yards for a first down or that its touchdowns should count for nine points? You'd say the team is dreaming and it's in for a bitter surprise when it has to play a real game.

Satan wants to encourage people to make up their own religion. He lies to them and says, "Go ahead—make up your own rules of right and wrong. There are no absolutes. Design a morality that is comfortable for you. Invent a game you think you can win."

Satan's helpers are doing a fabulous job in today's world, encouraging people to make up their own versions of truth. The truth is that God has made very clear His expectations for all human behavior, and anyone who tampers with His Word falls under special condemnation. St. John wrote, **"If anyone takes away from the words of the book of this prophecy, God will take away his share in the tree of life and in the holy city"** (Revelation 22:19).

How could we imperfect people design a game plan that is better than the all-knowing Lord of the universe? His perfect plan rescued us from eternal defeat. Jesus scored the win with His perfect life, innocent death, and amazing resurrection. God tells us that plainly in the Bible. If the Bible says it, that settles it.

June

The Lord God is a sun and shield. . . . Blessed is the one who trusts in You!

Psalm 84:11–12

June 1

Falling in Love

What could be more romantic than the notion of falling in love? We are all in love with the concept of love as an irresistible, magnetic force. We all love the romantic notion that there is that one special, magic person out there for us, and we all fantasize about being swept off our feet by that person.

Falling, however, means that you are out of control. Falling means that you may really hurt yourself—and others—when you land. **"King Solomon loved many foreign women . . . from the nations concerning which the Lord had said to the people of Israel, 'You shall not enter into marriage with them, neither shall they with you, for surely they will turn away your heart after their gods.' Solomon clung to these in love. . . . And his wives turned away his heart"** (1 Kings 11:1–3).

Our fallings and failings may never resemble King Solomon's, but we've had our own. Thank God that He forgives us for all the times that we've fallen and hurt ourselves or others. Fortunately, God does not let us stumble around to find out His will. He tells us.

Read Genesis 24 to find a better way. Abraham helped his son Isaac find a life partner who would reinforce his faith and keep him connected to the true God. Choosing to love is better than falling. We can love with our hearts—and our minds.

June 2

Repent and Return Now

When the *Titanic* struck an iceberg, it didn't sink right away. At first, people kept eating and drinking and dancing on the doomed vessel. Many slept right through the collision. Most could not believe the first reports of the coming disaster. "We were told this ship is *unsinkable*!"

The Lord warns us of the terrible destruction of Judgment Day not because He despises us, but because the universe is condemned, just like a sagging, rotting house. He is even now finalizing His plans for an entirely new world, and it is His passionate, fatherly desire to take us all there.

But first, our minds and hearts. It is urgent that we recognize the reason for God's judgment and accept responsibility for our part in it. The prophet Joel wrote, **"'Rend your hearts and not your garments.' Return to the Lord your God, for He is gracious and merciful, slow to anger, and abounding in steadfast love"** (Joel 2:13).

Repentant hearts welcome grace and mercy from their Savior, Jesus. Repentant hearts are not only spared God's anger, but are given wonderful promises. Interested in learning more about the great things God will do? Get into His Word.

June 3

You Are Valuable

Could the emotional atmosphere in your home stand some improvement? You know, people who criticize and abuse other people, including their nearest and dearest relatives, do it not because they feel powerful and in control. They make other people feel worthless because *they* feel worthless. That kind of negative talk just spirals down and down, making everything worse.

Jesus Christ came to our world to make things better. The Bible says in Colossians 3:12 that you are **"beloved"** by God. Wow! Apparently, you are valuable to God! He seems to think that you are worth a lot of effort to reclaim and restore.

As we experience Jesus' love, we will have some to share with the other wounded people around us, and that makes us a lot more fun to be with. Make it your mission today to make someone who lives in your home feel valuable.

Gentleness Is a Fruit of the Spirit

You have probably heard Jesus' famous words from the Sermon on the Mount about "turning the other cheek" (Matthew 5:38–39). That's terribly hard, isn't it? It certainly was hard for civil rights workers in the 1950s and 1960s. Dr. Martin Luther King, Jr.'s marchers down South found it really hard to be gentle when they were surrounded by whips, fire hoses, hatred, and violence. But civil rights came to black Americans not by guns and violence, but by love.

Here in the United States, it seems as though everybody admires people who are aggressive and abrasive. But you—let the Spirit of the Lord bring forth His holy fruit in you and lead you to gentle words and gentle actions today. Galatians 5:22–23 says that **"the fruit of the Spirit is . . . gentleness"** (actually, it's one of nine spiritual fruits). In other words, with your reborn willpower, you can choose to be humble and patient and to speak with a soft voice.

In this way, you will honor God; you will imitate Christ, your Savior and Leader; you will make other people's lives better; and as for you, you will find that you have a lot more friends.

June 5

The Gospel of Peace

Most military veterans will tell you that warfare is a marathon, not a sprint. Infantrymen move a lot, through rain, mud, dust, and snow. If you are going to move a lot, you had better have decent boots.

Guess what? Mobility is part of the arsenal of spiritual weapons given to you by God. The Bible says, **"Put on the whole armor of God. . . . and, as shoes for your feet, having put on the readiness given by the gospel of peace"** (Ephesians 6:11, 15).

In your Christian walk, you will go through many stressful changes. But what will sustain you in all the change, movement, and commotion of your life is the certain knowledge that Christ Jesus is your personal peace with God. You will also let God use you in the different places in the world that you have studied, lived, and worked.

Fathers Are Role Models

One of the features of life in families that suffer from a long history of poverty is that the children have no close family role models of people who have graduated from school and who go to work on time every day. God loves work. He does it every day Himself, and He designed His creatures to work too. God had Adam working all day *on his creation day* and *on his wedding day*, even *before* He introduced him to his beautiful wife, Eve.

There were men in the early Christian Church who were setting a poor example by their laziness and excuses. Paul had a better way: **"Aspire to live quietly, and to mind your own affairs, and to work with your hands . . . so that you may walk properly before outsiders and be dependent on no one"** (1 Thessalonians 4:11–12).

What's your example like—a good example, or a poor one? If it weren't for Jesus, we'd always be living with shortcomings and failures. He atoned for them all. His message of forgiveness is what motivates us to work with all our might.

Employers love employees with a strong work ethic. So do wives. And children desperately need to see a man in action in their lives who earns his bread, keeps his word, does good work, takes pride in his home, and knows how to finish a job.

Use the Buddy System

Mountain climbers never work alone—they always climb in groups. The buddy system has saved many, many lives. Your friend can help you when you slip and fall or when you get giddy from altitude sickness or when you run out of food. The harness and ropes that bind the climbers together are a matter of life and death.

Know what? God has great blessings to give you through the fellowship of other believers. The Bible says, **"Let us not give up meeting together, as some are in the habit of doing, but let us encourage one another—and all the more as you see the Day approaching"** (Hebrews 10:25 NIV).

"Church people" are sometimes mocked as hypocritical phonies. But most congregations I've seen are God's helpful rest stops for weary travelers. They are warm networks of fellow sinners and fellow redeemed, real people who share encouragement, accountability, energy, and love. C'mon—let's go to church.

June 8

Trust Your Creator

"What, me worry?" For many years the goofy, gap-toothed mascot of *Mad* magazine had that slogan beneath his picture. We wish. The reality is that you know people who worry a lot. Maybe the chief worrier in your life is *you.* It's one thing to be concerned about the future. It's another to worry. Worry is fear—fear that you've been abandoned, fear that everything is unraveling, fear that God's throne is empty and His angels are gone.

God wants us to shine with confident light in our world. And you know what? The brightest light comes from the testimony of Christians who have suffered *but who still exude confidence.* The Lord Jesus Himself was sorely tempted at times to feel abandoned and alone, and yet He comforted His disciples with these promises: **"Do not be anxious about your life, what you will eat or what you will drink, nor about your body, what you will put on. . . . Which of you by being anxious can add a single hour to his span of life?"** (Matthew 6:25, 27).

Trusting God means that I am convinced that God's heart loves me, that His mind has good plans and a good outcome set up for me, and that His hands can reach right into my life to make good things happen for me. I'll be okay. You will be too.

Show Mercy

The great philosopher Frank Burns once said, "It's nice to be nice to the nice." Well! Any idiot can treat people the way they deserve. You don't need to be a Christian to pay people back in kind. It takes a gift of the Holy Spirit to treat people better than they deserve. The word for that kind of treatment is *mercy.*

The Bible says, **"Let us use [our gifts]: . . . the one who does acts of mercy, with cheerfulness"** (Romans 12:6, 8).

Showing mercy means remembering that we are only starving beggars, made rich by God's rich gifts to us. It means showing patience with others, just as God has shown great patience with us. Be a living sacrifice today—show mercy to someone! Who owes you? Which of the sinful fools around you is in your debt? Is there a relationship you can restore today?

And by the way, when you do it, notice Paul's description—do it *cheerfully.* You received mercy from God for free, with love, unconditionally. You can do no less.

There Will Be Wars and Rumors of War

Christians must not grow careless or sleepy, lest Jesus' return catch them unprepared to give an account for their lives. But you know, the opposite is just as bad—that we get so jumpy and certain that the world will end any minute that we stop planning and building and sharing the Word.

Jesus wanted His followers to know how to read the times. Three days before His death, He helped them plan for what to expect in their (and our) lives: **"You will hear of wars and rumors of wars. See that you are not alarmed, for this must take place, but the end is not yet. For nation will rise against nation, and kingdom against kingdom"** (Matthew 24:6–7).

There is a strong Utopian urge in people to want to believe in human progress and a coming age of peace. Actually, the natural state of sinful man is warfare, only occasionally broken by small stretches of civility and cooperation. Violence is a permanent part of life on earth. It will touch you. Heads up.

Protect God's Reputation

When I was a teenager, one of my father's hardest jobs was to get me to think about others, to think in advance about the impact that my words and actions would have on other people. Now that I am a father, I have the joy of helping my teenagers learn that they are not sovereign and independent entities. They are *connected* to family, friends, school, church, employer . . . and God.

The God who created us and redeemed us has adopted us into His family. His Spirit now dwells within us as His temple. He claims us, and that means He also has high expectations of us. Paul wrote, **"You are not your own, for you were bought with a price. So glorify God in your body"** (1 Corinthians 6:19–20).

Wherever you go, you go as a publicly identified child of God. You carry the family name. Everything you say or do affects God's reputation. Now you know why Jesus thought it so important to train us to pray, "Hallowed be Your name." What will you show and tell the world about God today?

June 12

Head for the Finish Line

Ever wonder, "What am I doing here?" Maybe you're a husband trapped in a long afternoon of shopping with your wife. Maybe you're a wife trapped in a long evening of sports television at someone else's home. Maybe you're a teenager trapped in a visit to relatives and no one is your age.

You know what's worse? Wondering what you are doing on earth in the first place. A distressingly high percentage of people I've met have no clue that their lives have—or should have—a purpose. They drift through life and wonder why nothing satisfies in the long run.

There's a better way. Do you know where you are going? Do you see the finish line? Paul has some words of inspiration for you: **"One thing I do: forgetting what lies behind and straining forward to what lies ahead, I press on toward the goal for the prize of the upward call of God in Christ Jesus"** (Philippians 3:13–14).

The purpose of my life is not to get rich, get famous, or get pleasure. The purpose of my life is to get close to my Savior, Jesus, and give Him glory. What finish line are you heading for?

Choose Good Friends

"He fell in with bad company." "He was in the wrong place at the wrong time." "She just found herself in a situation." Ever heard talk like that? While seeming to get the young person off the responsibility hook, what it actually says is that the young person really chose some bad friends.

The people you choose to hang with eventually shape your character. You will start to talk like them, think like them, act like them. Proverbs 13:20 says, **"Whoever walks with the wise becomes wise, but the companion of fools will suffer harm."** Parents who aggressively choose good playmates for kids when they are small and who make a point of having their kids' high school friends around greatly decrease their children's chances of ever standing in a police lineup, becoming addicted to drugs, or making babies they can't raise.

On the other hand, choosing Christian friends makes it much more likely that kids' problems will find Christian solutions, that kids' views of life will be God's views, and that love and forgiveness received through Jesus will be on display in their lives. Do you know who your real friends are?

June 14

Honor Marriage

How's your life? Are you happy? Got some issues? How's your love life doing? One great happiness wrecker in the human experience is buying into Satan's lie that having sex outside of marriage is exciting and fulfilling. Actually, it just multiplies lying, sexually transmitted diseases, and unwanted children.

The Bible says in Hebrews 13:4, **"Let marriage be held in honor among all, and let the marriage bed be undefiled, for God will judge the sexually immoral and adulterous."**

You've got enough problems in your life without having God judging you. Want to make your life better today? Take care of the physical and emotional needs of your spouse.

The culture and society in which we live no longer helps you keep sexuality in marriage. The only reinforcement you will receive to honor God in this way is to be in the Word and to be with people who are in the Word so the Holy Spirit can strengthen your faith in Christ and guide you in your life.

June 15

A Kind Word to Others

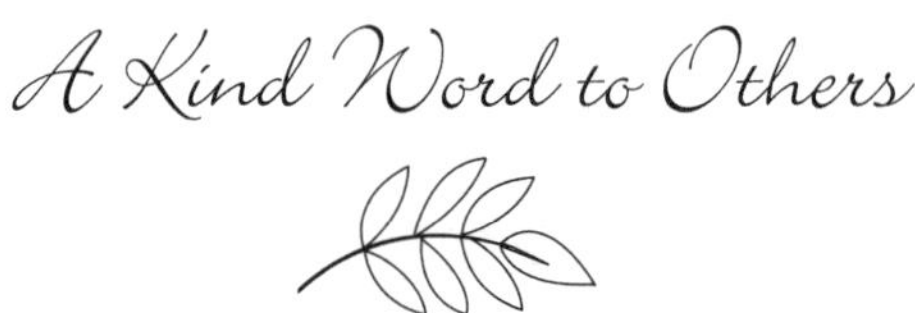

How I love kind words from other people! Kind words bandage up my wounds. They give me hope when my day has been bleak. They restore my self-confidence when I have been crushed. They make me feel as though I'm valuable when I have been feeling worthless.

You know, I don't need any personal training in how to lap up praise. Where I could use improvement is in building other people up. It is slowly dawning on me that one of the reasons for my earthly existence is to be an encourager. I need your praise, and you need mine.

Paul, once a persecutor of Christians, became a masterful recruiter and encourager of others: **"Let no corrupting talk come out of your mouths, but only such as is good for building up, as fits the occasion, that it may give grace to those who hear"** (Ephesians 4:29).

Once Paul came to know Jesus as his Redeemer, his whole life changed. With God's gift of grace, Paul discovered what it meant to serve others.

Ready? Let's practice: "Nice job!" "Love your hair." "Don't worry—you'll get it next time." "Great outfit!" "Thank you for everything you do around here." All of a sudden, you'll wonder why you have so many friends.

June 16

Rejection

I don't know about you, but one of the biggest feeders of the feeling of self-hatred in my own heart is rejection. I still remember keenly every one of the girls who didn't want to go out with me in my youth. And here's the reason for that secret pain. It's not that I'm not angry with them; I never was. I don't blame them at all. In fact, I fear that they were right. I fear that I am boring, ugly, and too big a loser to be seen with in public.

Surely you know the taste of rejection: cut from the team; dumped by your girlfriend or wife; fired from your job (which not only cuts off your income, but devastates your self-worth and even your identity); mocked and ignored by your children.

Rejection will be a part of human life until the end. That's why it's so important for all of us to tap into a steady and unlimited stream of affection and approval from our Savior-God: **"For my father and my mother have forsaken me, but the Lord will take me in"** (Psalm 27:10).

If I choose to let God be the ultimate arbiter of my self-worth, then I will never have to see myself as a loser. Faith in my Savior, Jesus, makes me a winner.

Equally Loved and Redeemed

Without a doubt, racial hatred is one of the greatest problems that has plagued our country since its inception. Thomas Jefferson wrote, "We hold these truths to be self-evident, that all men are created equal," but 175 years later, Hank Aaron was still not allowed to sleep with the rest of his team in a "white" hotel.

At its heart, racism is the conviction that somehow I am better and my tribe is worthier than other people. Therapy for the sick notion can begin with the truth that God loves all His creatures equally.

The Bible says in Acts 10:34–35, **"God shows no partiality, but in every nation anyone who fears Him and does what is right is acceptable to Him."** This truth helped a Jewish fisherman (Peter) and an Italian military commander (Cornelius) accept each other as brothers, and it will help you find love for racial reconciliation in your life. Satan helps you hate. Christ helps you accept, love, and respect.

June 18

Keeping God's Temple Healthy

Everyone pigs out once in a while—like at a family feast or a huge personal celebration. Eating gets out of balance, however, when we can't stop. When we consistently eat more than we are burning off, we begin slowly to destroy our temples. Carrying excess weight wears out joints prematurely, invites diabetes, unnecessarily burdens the heart, and clogs arteries with globs of fat and cholesterol.

Gluttony (living to eat—counting the minutes to the next meal) has long been recognized by Christians as one of the seven "deadly sins." We must all cultivate self-control in how we use our mouths to *talk*. But mouth self-control applies also to *eating*.

"Whether you eat or drink, or whatever you do, do all to the glory of God" (1 Corinthians 10:31). Begin and end your meals with prayer. Welcome your food as God's answer to your cries for daily bread. If you've given in to the temptations to misuse food, be assured of God's forgiveness and look to Him for strength as you develop the habits and discipline to control what you put in. Get help if you can't do it by yourself. God doesn't demand that all His children be skinny, but He does want you to eat to be healthy. Your body, after all, is the temple of the Spirit.

June 19

The Brokenness of Addiction

When they hear the word *addict,* most people first picture the image of a junkie, slowly destroying himself with a needle. Really, though, there are many kinds of addictions. People are chained to all kinds of destructive, compulsive behaviors—eating disorders, adulterous or homosexual sex, drugs, gambling, and many more. Some people don't know how to stop; others have lost their desire to stop. All compulsive, sinful lifestyles are bad and have the ability to keep people from their Savior.

What to do? Realize first of all that Jesus loves addicted people unconditionally. Who more than an addict can appreciate God's grace? Before an addicted person can believe in himself or herself again, it sure helps to realize that God thinks he or she is worth saving.

Second, God refuses to let people think that their situations are hopeless. Paul wrote, **"How can we who died to sin still live in it? . . . For sin will have no dominion over you, since you are not under law but under grace"** (Romans 6:2, 14). God and His Word and Supper are mightier than your compulsions, and His arms are long enough to reach down into your pit, no matter how deep you've dug it. It's never too late—come back to Daddy's arms today!

Stars

Do you live in a city like I do? If you do, you find that the stars are almost invisible because of light pollution from streetlights and neon signs. But when we urban dwellers get out to the country on a clear night, we have a "wow" moment. Know what I mean?

What do you make of the stars? These bright diamonds studding the velvety dark give silent beauty even to the night.

They are also symbols of God's faithfulness in carrying out the plan of salvation for the world. He once told Abraham, **"Look toward heaven, and number the stars, if you are able to number them. . . . So shall your offspring be"** (Genesis 15:5). Know what? His plan worked. Abraham's children, the believers with him in the divine promises, now truly number in the billions.

So next time you feel shaky in your faith, head out of town, pull off to the side of the road, and look up. You will see billions of reasons to trust in God's power.

June 21

Pain Demands Change

Much as I'd like to blame other people or even God for my problems, I have to admit that some of the pain in my life is self-inflicted. How about you?

Do a pounding head and hangover nausea in the morning remind you that your drinking last evening was stupid? Is your marriage turning sour because of poor choices on your part? Have you ever lost a job because of your own carelessness or arrogance or been broke because of your out-of-control spending? Have you tried to take sinful shortcuts to happiness and gotten burned?

Sin never satisfies long term. Satan sees to it that sinning often brings a short-term burst of excitement. But sooner or later, the pain comes, the pain that demands that something change. We usually think that all pain is bad. God thinks pain is good if it teaches us things we need to learn and if it softens up hard heads and hard hearts.

King David hurt himself often during his life, but he learned some valuable lessons, and he shared them with us. He wrote, **"My wounds stink and fester because of my foolishness. . . . But for You, O Lord, do I wait"** (Psalm 38:5, 15).

June 22

Let Go

"I'm really sorry, Mom," she apologized, as she picked up the broken candy dish that her toddler had accidentally demolished. "No problem," Grandma said lightheartedly. "I can always get another one." The younger woman's jaw dropped as she wondered, "Who is this woman? She sure is different from the days when *I* was the one breaking her stuff."

To all people who claim to be Christians, Colossians 3:8 says, **"Now you must put them all away: anger, wrath, malice."** As we get older, we learn the beautiful skill of letting go of poisonous emotions. We learn how to sort out what is truly valuable and what is of little value. Jesus' life and death addressed the poison problem each one of us carries around. Through daily repentance, we ask God to wash that poison away.

With the senior years comes the certainty that eternity is close at hand. Perhaps that awareness is what inspires grandparents to exercise greater tenderness with their grandkids than they managed to show their own kids.

Hey—this means you too! What poisonous emotions need to be drained from your heart today?

June 23

Get Some Rest

Just about everybody knows it's bad to be lazy. You know the Bible's law about no work, no eat, right? Well, the opposite is just as bad. Workaholics can do real damage to themselves and their families. People who endlessly feel guilt about downtime need to be given permission to rest.

The Lord Jesus Himself went on at least four retreats so He could rest up and recharge for the rigors of His ministry and the final ordeal. He took the opportunity to sleep when His body needed refreshing, even when the storm-tossed disciples thought He should have stayed awake: **"[Jesus] was in the stern, asleep on the cushion"** (Mark 4:38).

You know what happens to the machines in your life when you don't maintain them. Your body is a sacred trust from God. Take care of yourself. It's okay to delegate. It's okay to leave some things for tomorrow. It's okay to let God run things overnight. Practice letting go every day. Close your eyes without guilt. Let God refresh you at His Table.

June 24

Share Your Faith

When Satan fails to stop you from becoming a Christian, he switches to Plan B. He tries to make your faith and witness as invisible and ineffective as possible so that no one else will be infected with Christianity. He tells lies like "Your faith is purely personal and private. It is nobody's business what you believe."

What nonsense! Jesus gave His life for you and gave your faith to you in order to *share.* Jesus said to the believers in Matthew 5:13–14, **"You are the salt of the earth. . . . You are the light of the world."**

Spiritual salt and light can only do their jobs when they connect with other people. Salt makes people thirsty for the water of life—Jesus. Light helps people see where they really are and where the safe path lies.

You are a Christian today probably because of the witness of other believers. Who will claim you in heaven as salt and light?

June 25

Reflect on God's Forgiveness

Inside every person is the tank in which our emotions are stored. We have only a limited capacity for emotion, and if anger is using up most of that capacity, it will take very little to make us erupt into all kinds of mean and cruel words.

Want things to be better? The Bible says in Colossians 3:13, **"[Bear] with one another and, if one has a complaint against another, [forgive] each other; as the Lord has forgiven you."** In other words, the more you reflect on the cross of Jesus and God's huge forgiveness for you, the more you will be inclined to let go of your anger toward the fools and sinners around you. God's love makes us lovers. God's mercy makes us merciful.

You are not destined to be an angry person. You can choose to release your anger, just as you can drain a tank of its contents. You can learn to forgive. *Sí, se puede.* Yes, you can.

June 26

Playing with Fire

Spiritually weak people easily confuse lust with true love. Feeling a powerful attraction to someone else when you're married or to someone else who's married is a dangerous flirtation, not real love. People today seem to think that "being in love" justifies any and every action—cohabitation, dating married people, whatever. That powerful attraction must be obeyed and makes the sinful action "right."

God calls it playing with fire. **"Can a man carry fire next to his chest and his clothes not be burned? Or can one walk on hot coals and his feet not be scorched? So is he who goes in to his neighbor's wife; none who touches her will go unpunished"** (Proverbs 6:27–29).

People caught up in the rush of sinful sexual attraction often suffer from cessation of brain function. That's where you come in. Be a true friend. Tell them the truth. Lead them to recognize that they're playing with fire. Assure them of God's love in Jesus. Help the people in your world come to respect marriage again.

June 27

Idolatry is Blind

I don't believe I have ever heard anyone say, "Well, today I worshiped my idol again." Idolatry is a severe human problem. God used the very first of His Ten Commandments to forbid it. But the essence of idolatry is that people are absolutely convinced that they are trusting and confiding in something true and rock solid. Idolatry is always blind, which means that you might be hip deep in it right now.

An idol is the controlling force, the decision-making factor in your life. Do you need your boyfriend more than God? Is your money more precious than your divine forgiveness? Is your life organized around acquiring and using drugs or alcohol?

Wrong: "I know this is bad for me, but I need it to survive." Wrong: "I know my parents would disapprove of how I'm living right now, but if I don't, I'll lose my girlfriend." Right: **"The Lord God is a sun and shield. . . . Blessed is the one who trusts in You!"** (Psalm 84:11–12).

Whatever is keeping you from giving your whole heart, mind, body, soul, and spirit to the one true God is an idol and must go. Today would be a good day to get rid of it!

June 28

God Lives in Me

Anybody who has ever seen science fiction or horror movies gets the creeps thinking about being possessed by a spirit. True enough—possession by an evil spirit is horrible. The Bible gives us some dreadful examples of what demon possession does to people.

But having God the Holy Spirit living in you is a beautiful thing. The Lord Jesus loved His disciples so much that He promised the personal indwelling of God Himself in each believer.

He said, just hours before He died for us, **"I will ask the Father, and He will give you another Helper, to be with you forever, even the Spirit of truth. . . . You know Him, for He dwells with you and will be in you"** (John 14:16–17). Think of it—a loving God Himself lives in you to help you each day of your life.

You have a Friend. An Encourager. A Guide. A Power Source. A Teacher. How cool is that?

June 29

God Knows Me Inside Out

The longer you're married, the harder it is to bluff your way through life. My wife knows most of my dodges and cons. She can see through me like a pane of glass. She rolls her eyes at my dumb jokes and corrects my self-serving stories when I embellish them a little too much.

How do you feel about the idea that God knows every thought in your head, every secret in your heart, every deed in your past, and hears every word from your mouth, spoken, shouted, or mumbled? Isn't that a little intimidating? How can you hold your head up in church? How can you not feel dirty in His presence?

If God knows what a bluffer and faker you really are, can He like you? King David wrote about the concept of God's knowing him inside and out: **"O Lord, You have searched me and known me. . . . [You] are acquainted with all my ways"** (Psalm 139:1, 3).

It is the cleansing blood of Christ that takes away our fear. It is the cleansing blood of Christ that makes God's closeness a feeling of safety and security. He knows you. He likes you anyway.

June 30

Happiness Comes from God

It's relatively easy for us to see the sin of materialism in other people. When parents watch their kids opening birthday presents, sometimes they wince to see how quickly their children descend into gloating, bragging, and fighting over the toys. But big people are not immune. Satan lies to us constantly, telling us that happiness comes from getting what we want, in acquiring things, in getting our agendas done.

Grown-ups gloat, brag, and fight too. We envy and resent. Sometimes we feel proud, and sometimes we feel cheated.

The truth is that true happiness and satisfaction come from trusting in God, serving Him, and serving people. The Bible says in Philippians 3:8, **"I count everything as loss because of the surpassing worth of knowing Christ Jesus my Lord. For His sake I have suffered the loss of all things."**

Practice saying that passage five times. Mean every word.

July

We know that for those who love God all things work together for good.

Romans 8:28

July 1

The Lord Is Sovereign

Thomas Jefferson and some of the other founders of the United States were deists. They believed that God was active in creating the world but that He then disengaged. In modern times, He was only watching the world and, therefore, not acting in it.

You probably know people who see absolutely no evidence that God interacts with the world today. Perhaps you've had moments when you doubted that God saw your needs or got involved.

God has a different view. Psalm 103:19 says, **"The Lord has established His throne in the heavens, and His kingdom rules over all."** That means the Lord is sovereign. He acts. He is managing and steering and guiding all the world's events to benefit His believers. He is sovereign over sin, death, hell, and over Satan and all his demons. His plans will all be fulfilled, and He reigns supreme. The best part is that this sovereign King is your Father, who is using His power for you.

In heaven He will let you see everything He has been doing for you. Sometimes He lets you peek early.

The Fellowship of Believers

"It is not good for the man to be alone," said God as He created the first woman. It still isn't good for people to be isolated. He made us to be social creatures. He also created the concept of the Church because it is not good for people to be in spiritual isolation.

Satan has an easier time picking off the strays. Left to ourselves, we can get lost, consume things not good for us, and fall prey to any one of the thousand or so temptations that the devil has found successful in destroying people's bodies and souls.

"They devoted themselves to the apostles' teaching and the fellowship, to the breaking of bread and the prayers" (Acts 2:42). Every one of those divine activities builds up people's faith and spiritual strength. Every one is a gift from God, intended to be enjoyed by a spiritual family.

I need my Christian friends. I need someone to tell me if I'm getting weird in my beliefs. I need someone to tell me if I am rationalizing a sinful lifestyle. I need encouragement when I am down and a posterior kick when I am being stubborn. So do you. Do you have a congregation? Love it! Do you need a congregation? Find one!

Good Comes from Suffering

The Union soldiers who fought in the American Civil War experienced some unbelievable hardships. They fought in mud, bitter cold, and near starvation. But what sustained them was the knowledge that they were saving the country and helping to end slavery in America.

Have you had a hard life? You know, suffering is bad enough. But what makes pain really unbearable is when it seems to have no point—when no good seems to come of it.

One of the things I love about God is that He makes the sufferings of His children work for them. The Bible says in Romans 8:28, **"We know that for those who love God all things work together for good."**

This is an amazing promise. "All things" means *all things.* God works it both ways. He blesses you by giving you things and by subtracting. He blesses you by pampering you and depriving you. He blesses you with pleasure and with pain. He is working it all to get you to the finish line with your faith in Christ intact.

July 4, Independence Day

Let God Right the Wrongs and Fix Injustices

One of the great delights of living in the United States is that we all heartily agree with the Declaration of Independence that we are endowed with the rights to life, liberty, and, especially, the pursuit of happiness. Although everybody pursues happiness, so few people actually seem to find it.

The main reason is that they are looking in the wrong places. For instance, everybody grieves at injustice and wants revenge. You've heard the advice "Don't get mad, get even." A thousand books and plays and movies have their plots built on the central idea of revenge.

Revenge may briefly feel good, but it leads only to the injured person planning his own revenge. God says in Romans 12:17–19, **"Repay no one evil for evil. . . . 'Vengeance is Mine, I will repay.'"**

It is a relief to let God right the wrongs and fix the injustices, even if it never happens in our lifetime. He will take care of all injustice in His own time, and He will get it right.

You know, I feel better already.

July 5

There Will Be Famines and Earthquakes

One of the sadder outcomes of Adam and Eve's rebellion is that all of nature is out of whack. The beautiful world that God made as our home now fights with farmers who must wrest a harvest from dry, thorny ground by their own sweat. In Eden, all of nature was paradise. Now our world goes crazy occasionally, unleashing enormous blasts of destructive energy. Tsunamis, hurricanes, avalanches, earthquakes, and tornadoes strike suddenly, and they destroy and kill.

And then there is the slow death of drought and famine. In Eden, water distribution was predictable and consistent. For millennia now, rainfall and snowmelt have been erratic and sometimes completely absent. Crops shrivel. Animals wither. People can die.

Expect these things, says Jesus. **"There will be famines and earthquakes in various places. All these are but the beginning of the birth pains"** (Matthew 24:7–8). Someday these disasters will be no more. For now, they are part of our environment.

July 6

Expect God's Blessings

People get down when they feel that all their efforts are wasted and pointless. They get cynical and say things like "Virtue is its own punishment" and "No good deed goes unpunished." We think we know too many stories about how cheaters prosper and the violent win.

That's just bitter talk. Blind too. The Bible says that the Lord **"blesses the dwelling of the righteous"** (Proverbs 3:33). And it promises that **"you will walk on your way securely. . . . When you lie down, your sleep will be sweet"** (Proverbs 3:23–24). The Lord pays attention. He remembers. And then He acts.

The word *bless* means that God intervenes in our lives to make them better. He accepted the obligation of fatherhood when we were washed with water and the Word. He promised to make good things happen to the righteous. When things are right with you and God, your sleep is sweet indeed.

July 7

He Has Revealed Himself

There are some areas of human knowledge that are completely over my head. I know nothing of mathematical analysis or calculus. You can talk about it all day, and I won't get a word.

Some people never studied a foreign language. They hear French or Arabic and hear only babbling, meaningless syllables.

Here is another example of how much God loves you: He gave you the plan of salvation in words you can understand, remember, and speak. The Bible says in Romans 10:8–9, "**'The word is near you, in your mouth and in your heart,' . . . [I]f you confess with your mouth that Jesus is Lord and believe in your heart that God raised Him from the dead, you will be saved.**"

Ponder with me how awesome a gift is our language. Long before you are allowed to see Him face-to-face, Christ Himself comes to you through words.

July 8

I Do; I Will

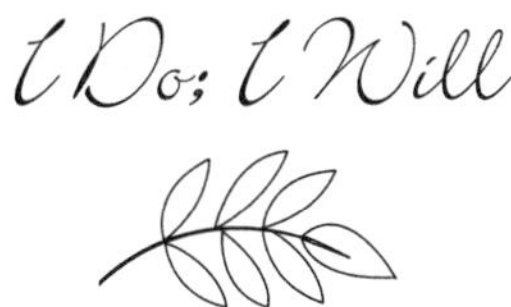

One of the reasons we watch movies and consume sports is that we are all hungry for heroes. We all crave role models to help us know how to act in life. The public is also hungry for details of celebrities' lives because they set the tone for our value systems.

The most important human value that we all need—and need to show—is *love.* But you will not find much real love on the big screen. Real love is not a mindless glandular response. Real love is a decision one person makes to sacrifice of himself or herself to make someone else's life better. It's at the cross of Christ where you will find the purest example of the true love that we all need and crave. Christ is the hero and example that we must follow.

"Husbands, love your wives, as Christ loved the church and gave Himself up for her, that He might sanctify her" (Ephesians 5:25–26). Note that Jesus didn't just say, "I *do* love you." He also promised, "I *will* love you." True Christ-love is a decision and a promise. That is what a godly man will promise his wife and vice versa.

July 9

As the United States continues its war on terrorism, military leaders are constantly preparing troops and weapons for and against attacks. Humvee™ trucks in the Middle East now carry a considerable amount of armor to defend against explosive devices. Soldiers wear Kevlar® fiber body armor to protect vital organs.

St. Paul wants Christians to know that they also are under spiritual attack from Satan and his demons from hell. It is Satan's chief objective to destroy your faith and separate you from your heavenly Father.

In Ephesians 6:13, Paul urges us to **"take up the whole armor of God, that you may be able to withstand in the evil day, and having done all, to stand firm."**

With truth wrapped around your waist, Christ's righteousness covering your hearts, feet ready to walk for God, the shield of faith around you, salvation protecting your head, and the sword of God's Word in your hand, you will be ready for any assault—and ready also to carry out your sacred mission in life.

God's Personal Interest in Me

Bob Seger has a song that tells about being a nobody and feeling like a number. Do you know that song? Do you know that feeling? The world has many, many ways of making you feel insignificant and unimportant.

One of the things I love about God is that He takes a personal interest in me, little me. And He's not merely watching me, but He actually intervenes in my life at just the right times to make it better.

The Lord says to you and me in Psalm 50:15, **"Call upon Me in the day of trouble; I will deliver you, and you shall glorify Me."** This little sentence contains a string of powerful promises: God hears when you cry out to Him. God cares when you cry out to Him. God acts when you cry out to Him.

Call Him up today. He is standing by.

July 11

We Are All Created Equal

"Can we all get along?" This was the plea of Rodney King, the man beaten by Los Angeles police officers, as he looked at wreckage from the riot that followed the officers' acquittal. Can we indeed? I hope this is a question that you care about. Racism and racial hatred hurt all societies, ours included.

Racial hatred goes against the original intent of our Creator. When the Declaration of Independence states as one of the central philosophies of the brand-new United States of America that "all men are created equal," it is merely affirming what the Bible says in Acts 17:26: **"[God] made from one man every nation of [people]."**

We can get so caught up in our differences of geography, skin color, dialect, behavioral patterns, and culture that we forget our commonality. We are all equally sinful under the holy law of God. We are all equally loved by our Creator and equally redeemed by the blood of Christ. Because of Christ, we are members of the family of God. And we are united with Him in water and Word. Most important, we are members of the Body of Christ.

But we are also all members of the same divinely created race—the human race.

July 12

Fatigue

Thanks to Satan, trusting in God is a challenge even when things are going well. Think how much harder it is to feel confident when you're exhausted. "Good tired" is how you feel at the end of a productive day. But you probably also know "bad tired," don't you? "Bad tired" is when you are physically and emotionally drained by the selfishness of others or, worse yet, by your own foolishness and bad judgment.

Are you the parent of a newborn who won't let you sleep? Do you sit up in the dark, waiting for your teenagers to come home? Have you spent yourself into some serious debt? Do problems at work give you insomnia? Are you fried by trying to work and go to school and manage a family all at the same time?

Fatigue wears down your cheerfulness and patience. Fatigue breeds pessimism and bitterness. The Lord Jesus knew personally what severe exhaustion felt like, and He wanted His tired brothers and sisters to know that there was relief for them. He said, **"Come to Me, all who labor and are heavy laden, and I will give you rest"** (Matthew 11:28).

As you lay your head on the pillow tonight, say this prayer: "Lord, You are big enough to handle everything on my mind right now. Since You're going to be up all night anyway, I'd like You to work on some things that are bothering me. I'm ready now for the sweet rest You promised."

Pleasant dreams!

July 13

God Controls the Holy Angels

One of the greatest things about living in the United States is that I feel that I can trust our military to be working for me. Although I don't see soldiers very often, I know that they are on duty, protecting our country.

I sleep even better knowing that God's army of angels is on duty as well. My heavenly Father, who loves me, has promised that these powerful creatures are working to serve and protect—serve and protect *me.* Wow! Someday I will find out all the things that they were doing for me, but for now, I rejoice in the promise of Psalm 91:11 that **"[God] will command His angels concerning you to guard you in all your ways."**

The Bible tells some amazing stories about what angels did to help God's people. They rescued Abraham's nephew Lot from a mob. They inflicted the final plague on Egypt, freeing the Israelites from slavery. They surrounded God's lonely prophet Elisha with hills full of horses and chariots of fire, thrilling and comforting him.

Those same angels are still at work for you.

July 14

Your Enemy Is a Beast

The news gets grimmer. You have not only one enemy but many. Satan's fellow fallen angels, often called "demons," hate you too. What's more, Satan has deceived certain human agents and has persuaded them to follow his terrible agenda.

Sometimes Satan's human agents manage to achieve high government or military power, and they use that power to attack and hurt believers. The Bible calls satanic governmental or military power **"a beast rising out of the sea. . . . [The beast] was allowed to make war on the saints and to conquer them. And authority was given it over every tribe and people and language and nation. . . . Here is a call for the endurance and faith of the saints"** (Revelation 13:1, 7, 10).

Believers have suffered terrible persecutions from the beastly governments that were supposed to protect them. Even today, in these "enlightened times," Christians are being harassed, arrested, imprisoned, beaten, and even killed by the beast. Be alert and don't be surprised. But know this: the beast cannot touch your eternal salvation, and the blood of Christian martyrs only makes our Savior look more wonderful to those who remain.

July 15

God Intervenes for You

Where are You, God?" Every thinking believer has whispered that desperate prayer at least once, and some have said it many times. A large part of our human dilemma is that God, in judgment, gave Adam and Eve and their descendants part of what they said they wanted—freedom from Him. So He withdrew, at least visibly. People no longer heard His voice or "footsteps" in their gardens.

Until the birth of Christ, that is. An older priest named Zechariah was ecstatic that God Himself was coming, *in person,* to rescue humanity from the ancient curses: **"Blessed be the Lord God of Israel, for *He has visited* and redeemed His people"** (Luke 1:68, italics added).

God Himself, in the person of Jesus Christ, again walked the earth. People once again heard the voice of God, and the voice brought good news. You can trust a God who keeps His promises and who came in person to finish the job.

July 16

God Guides the Nations

On the face of it, you can understand why people think that God has lost interest in managing human history. Today we fret over World War III breaking out in the Middle East, and we live with the threat of global terrorism. Law and order are breaking down everywhere as people seem to go berserk with violence.

Yet our loving God chooses to stay engaged with His world, not only on the *micro* level—with you personally—but also on the *macro* level, with the rise and fall of nations. When you're feeling panicky that the world is out of control, let the prophet Isaiah's promise reassure you: **"This is the purpose that is purposed concerning the whole earth, and this is the hand that is stretched out over all the nations. For the Lord of hosts has purposed, and who will annul it?"** (Isaiah 14:26–27).

Over and over, the Old Testament prophets assured little Israel that their Lord was the Lord of the nations. From Egypt to Persia, from mighty Babylon to mighty Rome, He lifted them up and brought them down to make His agenda happen.

He still does. Relax.

July 17

Children, Show Respect

Aretha Franklin was right—everybody needs respect. We are all half-starved for lack of respect. Hunger for respect is what drives young men to join gangs. It's what motivates people to work obscenely long hours at their jobs or to feel driven to stack up university degrees after their names.

Now, kids, here's the secret. To get respect, you first give it. Obviously, respecting God Himself comes first. In second place come parents. It's no coincidence that the very first of the Ten Commandments to deal with human relationships speaks to parental respect: **"Honor your father and your mother, that your days may be long in the land that the Lord your God is giving you"** (Exodus 20:12).

Get it? God solemnly promises to increase both the quantity and the quality of your life when you lift up your parents in your heart and show them honor in the way you treat them. He also promises to make your life harder when you dishonor them.

Today is the day. You are the one. How can you honor your heavenly Father by honoring your earthly parents today?

God's Justice Is Perfect

Some parents teach their children a sense of justice in which rewards follow good deeds and punishments follow bad deeds. What really disturbs children is when the guilty go unpunished. They feel violated, whether it's because of the actions of a playground bully or of a terrorist.

Sad to say, human justice often doesn't get done.

Ah, but the Lord watches, remembers, and acts. Even if our justice system is imperfect, sometimes punishing the innocent and failing to punish the guilty, God's justice is perfect. Sooner or later, He will take care of business. Psalm 11:6–7 says this about God and His justice: **"Let Him rain coals on the wicked; fire and sulfur. . . . The LORD is righteous; He loves righteous deeds; the upright shall behold His face."**

This is why Christians can exist and even flourish in an unjust world. Although our God wants all people to be in heaven with Him someday, and though He sent His Son for all people, some will reject Him. We are absolutely confident that God will take care of business in His time.

True Peace

"Peace, baby." Yikes. What a mindless slogan. When they were young, Baby Boomers used to greet each other with those words, two fingers up in the air. *Peace* may be one of the most overused and least-experienced concepts in the English language.

Real peace is more than just silence, more even than just the end of hostility. Real peace means that things are put right again, that truth and justice and goodness have prevailed. Real restoration of order and harmony are gifts from God. Paul wrote, **"The peace of God, which surpasses all understanding, will guard your hearts and your minds in Christ Jesus"** (Philippians 4:7).

God has declared you not guilty through the work of Christ. Do you know what that really means? God has no anger or condemnation toward those who believe in Christ. God actually likes you. A lot. What this means is that your insides can quiet down. It means that you don't have to dread the future. It means that your first face-to-face meeting with the Supreme Deity will be a thrilling family reunion.

Peace indeed.

Make a Declaration of Dependence on God

All Christians struggle with the idea that we sometimes have to suffer during our earthly lives. Admit it. You've been bothered by that, haven't you?

One of the good things that God can make happen through our pain is to deflate our arrogance and bring down our pride. All of us try so hard to be in control of our lives: we save money, we accumulate power, we plan and work—all to feel in control. Actually, it's not such a bad thing to realize how little we really control. We do need God—who *is* in control of all things—and we need Him more than anything in the whole world.

The Bible says in Acts 17:28, **"In Him we live and move and have our being."** Do you truly believe that? Let your times of suffering lead you to make a declaration of dependence on God.

July 21

Getting Some Exercise

Some of my ancestors were pioneer farmers in the Midwest. How they would have howled with laughter to see today's treadmills and stationary bicycles that never go anywhere. How they would laugh to see gyms with progressive-resistance machines and racks and racks of free weights. Before automobiles, you didn't need a treadmill for an aerobic workout. When you had grubbed out two or three tree stumps in a day, you didn't need to go home and pump iron.

That was then. Today God doesn't expect us all to be bodybuilders or marathon runners. But He does expect us to care for our bodies and maintain them—after all, they are a place of residence for Him and useful and necessary for the important role you play. Paul wrote, **"Do you not know that you are God's temple and that God's Spirit dwells in you? If anyone destroys God's temple, God will destroy him. For God's temple is holy, and you are that temple"** (1 Corinthians 3:16–17).

We are God's temple because of the new life Jesus gave us through His life, death, and resurrection. The Holy Spirit has taken up residence in us. We are His.

Appreciate your health. Keep that blood pressure down. Burn up everything you eat. We need you at full strength!

God Sees Everything

One of the most cherished rights of U.S. citizens is the right to privacy. Local, state, and federal governments cannot enter a home, seize property, or wiretap phone conversations without an explicit court warrant. Evidence that has been seized without proper procedures is inadmissible in court. Suspects must be read their Miranda rights, which include the right to remain silent.

Does it surprise you to know that you have absolutely no privacy rights with God? He is your Creator and Judge. Not only are your public deeds under His scrutiny, but He has the right to evaluate your words and even listen in on your thoughts. Psalm 11:4 says, **"The LORD is in His holy temple; the LORD's throne is in heaven; His eyes see, His eyelids test the children of man."** The whole world is accountable to God. The whole world is laid bare before His eyes. He sees and remembers everything. Everything.

The point? Don't squander precious time right now by planning on dodging responsibility to God by pleading expiration of the statute of limitations. Don't argue about freedom of speech and Miranda rights and privacy. Don't hope for access to a slick lawyer or trust in your own glib tongue. God sees. God knows. God remembers. You're busted.

It is just such people as you that Christ came to save.

July 23

God's Unconditional and Universal Love

Some of the most beautiful places and buildings in my city have signs on them restricting admittance. "Members only!" they read, or "Authorized personnel only!" You know why, of course. You have to pay to play at that level. If you don't have the wealth, you don't get in.

Aren't you glad that when your life ends, you won't have to face an exclusive heavenly club? Some people think they have to earn it. In fact, Jesus gives the tickets away.

One of the things I love about God is that His love is unconditional and universal. Jesus' death and resurrection bought forgiveness for the entire human race and opened up heaven to anyone who believes in Him. It's not about your performance. It's about Christ's.

The Bible says in 1 Timothy 2:3–4, **"God our Savior . . . desires all people to be saved and to come to the knowledge of the truth."** It will look like the United Nations gathered around God's throne. I love it!

July 24

I don't like money, actually, but it quiets my nerves." The Brown Bomber, boxer Joe Louis, said that to laughing reporters. The truth is that every last buck will be taken from us by force when death comes. Our heirs, lawyers, and government will get it all. If your money is your greatest treasure, prepare to be robbed big time.

Far more valuable than your cash is your faith in Christ. Even a small, weak faith in our big Savior will bring you forgiveness of your sins and adoption into the royal family of heaven.

That's why God sometimes lets you suffer economic reversals now—because He loves you too much to let you become a shortsighted candidate for hell. Financial hardships don't signify God's curse but, in fact, the reverse: **"These [trials] have come so that your faith—of greater worth than gold . . . may be proved genuine and may result in praise, glory and honor when Jesus Christ is revealed"** (1 Peter 1:7 NIV).

Say it with me: "If I have money but not Christ, I will end up with nothing. If I have Christ, I will inherit everything. My real wealth is waiting for me in heaven."

July 25

God Is Omniscient

Normally we don't like it when people think of themselves as being smarter than we are. We call them "know-it-alls," and that name is not meant as a compliment. Well, guess what? God is omniscient; He really *does* know it all. His mind is vast enough to track all the thoughts and actions of all the people on earth. His memory has enough RAM to remember all human history, small and great.

Psalm 139:1–2 says, **"O Lord, You have searched me and known me! You know when I sit down and when I rise up; You discern my thoughts from afar."** This has to terrify unbelievers. It means that they will never, *ever* get away with anything.

But those who believe they are forgiven in Christ will find the concept of an omniscient God greatly comforting. It means that we are worshiping a great big God. It means He won't forget to take care of us the way we forget to feed the fish and find them floating upside down. It means He remembers all His promises, keeps all His commitments, and won't ever lose track of a single one of us.

July 26

Pray for All the Saints

During the initial war against the Taliban in Afghanistan, the Afghan Northern Alliance troops used to marvel at how the U.S. missiles and bombs seemed to come out of nowhere. They would be studying enemy positions through high-powered binoculars and see bodies flying, even though they had not heard the artillery or seen the planes that delivered the ordnance.

Guess what? God has given you spiritual power that has a range even greater than that of a cruise missile. Through Christ, you can pray for anyone, anywhere on earth. Furthermore, you have unlimited minutes, and the same free rate applies not only to weekends and evenings, but to prime time as well.

The Bible says in Ephesians 6:18, **"[Make] supplication for all the saints."** What a thrill it is to know that God answers our prayers to help people we care about even when they may be ten thousand miles away. What a thrill it is to know that His communication center is open 24/7. What a thrill it is to know that He loves to hear from us, processes every request, and answers it *in the very best way*. Every time.

JULY 27

Integrity Builds Trust

Is compartmentalizing good? It's good if it means that guys sort all their tools and sports gear and keep everything in the proper bins and drawers. It's horrible if it means that they think they live in different worlds that have nothing to do with one another. It's horrible when a Christian man's faith does not influence his business ethics. It's horrible when a man professes loyalty to his wife at home and then plays with the females in his "other worlds."

The Bible calls that game "double-mindedness" and condemns it. **"That person must not suppose that he will receive anything from the Lord; he is a double-minded man, unstable in all his ways"** (James 1:7–8).

Double-mindedness in our own lives needs to be dealt with. We come to our gracious God both for His free forgiveness as well as His guidance for how to live our lives differently.

The antidote to compartmentalization of the mind is godly *integrity.* Integrity means that a man sees his whole life as connected, that it's all one. Promises made in one world apply in the others. And you know what? This is how trust is built. Know what else? Wives really love and respond to men they can trust.

Accepting Responsibility for Others

After you have become proficient at seeing how connected you are to others and taking care to bring joy instead of pain to them, you are ready for advanced Christianity. And that means accepting responsibility for others to whom you are connected.

On the surface of it, this seems to be both a real pain and also a significant risk of empowering and enabling bad behavior. Both of those concerns are real, not imaginary.

Christ's greatest work is rescuing unworthy sinners. He calls you to nothing less than that very same work. You are His hands, mouth, lap, and legs in seeking and saving. Listen to (and emulate) Paul's care and concern for a young man named Onesimus, who was struggling to live his faith: **"If he has wronged you at all, or owes you anything, charge that to my account. I, Paul, write this with my own hand: I will repay it"** (Philemon 18–19).

If we must err, let's err on the side of generosity and giving.

July 29

Heaven Is Beautiful

The great Italian actor and director Roberto Benigni won all kinds of awards for his film *Life Is Beautiful (La Vita è Bella)*. The title is bitterly ironic. The hero is an Italian Jew who was thrown into a Nazi prison camp with his little boy and was eventually shot. We all try our best to control our environments, but no matter how hard we try, the ugliness of sin and death breaks in.

The Bible says that life in heaven, the holy city, will be beautiful—for real! St. John was allowed to peek. He said, **"[It had] the glory of God, its radiance like a most rare jewel. . . . The city was pure gold, clear as glass"** (Revelation 21:11, 18).

God is the beauty of heaven, and what's amazing is that through the work of Christ on our behalf, He allows us to share His glory there forever. Our surroundings will be beautiful. We will be beautiful. *Il cielo è bello*—heaven is beautiful.

July 30

The Lord Our God is Holy

The ancient Greeks and Romans longed to connect with the great power of the world. They constructed for themselves an elaborate system of gods and goddesses whom they supposed had authority over the land, sea, sun, moon, and so on. But those gods and goddesses acted just like them—though big and powerful, they were jealous, petty, and vengeful.

How sweet it is for us to hear from the Bible that there is only one God and that He is holy and pure, without any trace of evil. Psalm 99:9 says, **"Exalt the Lord our God, and worship at His holy mountain; for the Lord our God is holy!"**

How could you worship someone just as rotten and corrupt as the powerful on earth? How could you trust someone who might just betray you for the fun of it? How could you respect as divine someone who is violent and out of control?

What a thrill it is to kneel before the holiness of the Lord God!

July 31

Celebrate God's Love

Here's a universal principle that's true for all mankind: people need love. We all live in a world awash in pain, hatred, fear, and self-loathing. We are all starved for affection and approval. What a joy it is to hear the Bible's message in Galatians 5:22 that **"the fruit of the Spirit is love."**

In other words, it is one of the Spirit's major working goals to bring God's love to you, plant it in your heart, and help you believe that you are somebody precious to the Lord. Lay your head on your pillow tonight absolutely certain that you are known, valued, and claimed.

Goal 2 is to inspire and empower you to love other people. God chose the term *fruit* to encourage you to see that you, in a sense, are God's orchard, and He expects you to treat other people the way He treats you.

Don't say, "I love everybody"—that's too vague. Pick one person in your life who seems most love-starved. Today's the day to bear some fruit.

AUGUST

My help comes from the Lord, who made heaven and earth.

Psalm 121:2

August 1

Leadership Is a Gift

People tend to have a love-hate relationship with their leaders. On one hand, they chafe under someone else's rules, nitpick decisions they don't like, and enjoy the ridicule leaders get from comedians. It's handy to have a leader around to blame for things you don't like.

On the other hand, people—all jokes aside—are hungry for good leadership, and they groan when it's bad. People need organization, communication, and, above all, inspiration and vision. Those things come from the Holy Spirit. Where would we be without the leadership and guidance of the Lord of the Church? I love being part of an organization that is well managed.

Good leadership doesn't just happen—it's one of the Spirit's gifts. The Bible says that **"if [someone's gift] is leadership, let him govern diligently"** (Romans 12:8 NIV).

Are you in charge of other people in some way? You have been placed there by God to bring benefit to others, not to serve yourself.

AUGUST 2

Future Possibilities

One of the most vicious of all human failings is our terrible capacity for holding grudges. Think of how many relationships we have wrecked by being obsessed with the past, with refusing to forgive, with holding people's failings over their heads long after the event.

God wants you to know that He is aware of your own personal failings. But Jesus has already paid off all your debts of the past and future. Imagine that! You are pre-forgiven!

God says in Jeremiah 31:34, **"I will forgive their iniquity, and I will remember their sin no more."**

What a relief to know that once you are forgiven, you stay forgiven. Love keeps no record of wrongs, and because God is love, *He* keeps no record of wrongs. God is much more interested in the possibilities of your future, because His grace is future oriented. He forgives you, not merely to help you avoid terrible condemnation in His court, but to help you grow into a person more useful for His work.

August 3

Hope During Loss

All of us have suffered and will suffer some more. All of us have struggled and will struggle some more. And here's something that we need to know: Did God notice? Did this count for anything? Is there any meaning in it? Did it matter?

Jesus has a simple answer: "Yes." The Father watches and keeps track of all of His children's hardships, and there is a sweet, divine reimbursement plan for us all. We will all be remembered and compensated in direct proportion to how much He has allowed us to be hammered during the time of our earthly combat.

Peter and the other disciples gave up a lot to follow Jesus. Peter once wondered out loud if their sacrifices and losses meant anything at all to God. Jesus assured him, **"I say to you, there is no one who has [suffered loss] for the sake of the kingdom of God, who will not receive many times more in this time, and in the age to come eternal life"** (Luke 18:29–30). Jesus Himself suffered more than anyone, and His ultimate sacrifice gives us the confident hope of eternal life.

Think about it: the Giver of everlasting life and the Controller of all the wealth of the universe refuses to be out-given by His children.

AUGUST 4

Passion for God

Who wants to hang around apathetic people? Not me! The people I most enjoy being with have fire in the belly for something. When the Spirit of the Lord is moving among people, He distributes passion, the inner burn that wants to change something for Jesus, who changed us from being spiritually dead to being spiritually alive!

God was once very pleased with a man who had served Him well: **"Phinehas son of Eleazar, the son of Aaron, the priest, has turned My anger away from the Israelites; for he was as zealous as I am for My honor among them"** (Numbers 25:11 NIV). From that day on, God channeled the priestly line through Phinehas's family.

Have you ever wondered about your purpose on earth—how you can serve your Lord in thanks for His service to you? What do you care about? Where does your passion lie? Do you love kids? music? counseling? planting? accounting? design? poetry? building things? Let 'er rip. Burn like Phinehas.

August 5

God Is Your Best Caretaker

I was visiting a convalescent home recently, a place, as they say, "for the aging." It struck me that there is a whole list of adjectives that nobody uses anymore: *aged*, *elderly*, and, especially, *old*. America apparently has no more "old" people. We are only "aging."

But, you know, it's okay to be old. That doesn't mean that you're washed up and useless. You are still part of God's earthly work force. Nor does it mean that everything is being taken from you. If you're a Christian, what it really means is that you're very, very close to seeing Jesus personally in heaven.

God is your best caretaker. In words especially dear to all the aging, Jesus said, **"Let not your hearts be troubled. . . . In My Father's house are many rooms. . . . I go to prepare a place for you"** (John 14:1–2).

You might call this a homecoming.

August 6

God Is on Your Side

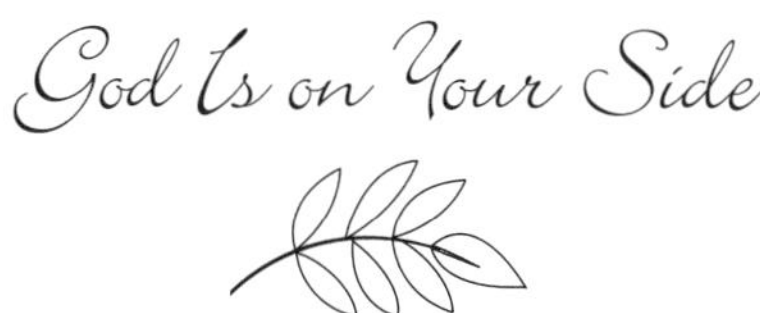

Do you ever find God's ways confusing? By now you've lived long enough to have been hurt many times. Sometimes you have to wonder if God is really working for you or against you.

English poet William Cowper's little 1773 poem on the puzzle of God's ways has been repeated countless times by hopeful believers: "God moves in a mysterious way His wonders to perform; He plants His footsteps in the sea And rides upon the storm" (*LSB* 765:1).

But that's one of the things that I have really come to love about God. As I get older, I see more and more that the Lord really knows exactly what He's doing in my life. He says in Jeremiah 29:11–12, **"I know the plans I have for you, . . . plans for welfare and not for evil, to give you a future and a hope. Then you will call upon Me and come and pray to Me, and I will hear you."**

It's a treat to live long enough to be allowed to see God's plans unfolding and to see that His plans are actually pretty good.

August 7

See Your Spouse As God's Gift

We live in the consumer age. Our fickle buying habits drive companies to pamper us with better and better products and services. Every year, hotels get better and computers get faster. Cable TV brings more channels and stores offer an ever-broader array of stuff.

If you look at your spouse with consumer eyes, you will soon be disappointed. This year's model may look a lot like last year's, definitely showing some wear. There is no money-back guarantee or customer service department. There is no one you can sue.

So *don't* look at your spouse with consumer eyes. Look with the eyes of faith, seen through the lens of God's Word. **"He who finds a wife finds a good thing and obtains favor from the Lord"** (Proverbs 18:22). Your loving God is blessing you by letting you be married—it's a sign of His favor, not a desire to torture you.

You can itemize the ways in which your spouse falls short—or you can take inventory of all your spouse's good qualities. That very attitude makes everything better. If your spouse feels judged and inadequate, he may just give up and live down to your low expectations. But if he feels appreciated, he will strive to live up to your words of praise.

Isn't it amazing that when we look at our spouse through the eyes of faith, we see much more clearly the blessings of God?

Loved by God

Have you ever looked at the personals section of a newspaper or magazine? Were you surprised by the huge number of personal ads? Don't be. God made us to be love sponges. All of us crave acceptance and community, affection and admiration.

We need all these things from God too. John wrote, **"In this is love, not that we have loved God but that He loved us and sent His Son to be the propitiation [atoning sacrifice] for our sins"** (1 John 4:10). True love goes first and initiates the relationship. Thanks to Jesus, you can know with certainty that you are precious to God, that you have great worth, that you are somebody. Jesus loves you!

One of the many ways that God shows His love to you is by putting people in your life who show love to you. Can you tell who they are? And guess what? You just might be God's agent to show love to *them.* Isn't it a privilege to be God's arms and smile to somebody else? Which weary sinner needs a hug from you today?

God's Work Revealed through Disability

Modern medicine, home health care, and skilled-care facilities are all wonderful things for people with major health problems. But one side effect of these things is they make people more invisible to the general public. Have you ever spent an afternoon in a nursing home? How many people do you know with Down syndrome?

Advocates for the disabled hate the term *disabled*; they prefer *differently abled.* The Americans with Disabilities Act puts the clout of the state behind the movement to make public buildings accessible. Excellent! We Christians should lead the pack in helping people define themselves not by what they *can't* do but by what they *can*.

Our Lord Jesus once explained why God had allowed a man to experience blindness for many years: **"that the works of God might be displayed in Him"** (John 9:3). Physical brokenness can work for God's loving plans if it makes us hungry for heaven; if it makes us kind and helpful to those weaker than we are; if it rebukes our chronic selfishness and materialism and draws us closer to Him. Is it possible that God lets you live with physical brokenness so that His work might be revealed in *your* life?

Getting Older Isn't So Bad

If supermarket magazines are any indicator, the aging process is a disaster in every way. Everybody pictured in them is young, healthy, and beautiful, and the stores offer you a thousand products to make you look younger—or make you *think* you look younger. The sad result of this relentless marketing is that people think that their worth and value diminish as they get older.

But the aging process has some real benefits. Along with wrinkles comes wisdom. With age, you can see how God works all things together for good for those who love Him. You can see His kindly purposes unfolding slowly over the decades. You accumulate friends, both on earth and in heaven. And you can see how He uses people as His partners in making good things happen.

Older people have learned much about money, people, and life. Job shared this observation: **"Wisdom is with the aged, and understanding in length of days"** (Job 12:12).

I'm looking forward to getting older! Especially since it gets me one step closer to my Savior in heaven.

August 11

The Spirit's Indwelling

Do you ever feel like a laboratory rat? Do you ever feel as though God, wearing His white lab coat and carrying a clipboard, is analyzing your performance to decide if you're worthy of your cheese? Or that you're struggling all alone in a hard and cruel game where the odds seem stacked against you?

Fear not. Your Creator is also your Savior. He cares intensely that you should succeed in your life. He gives you accurate *information* of His great victories in language that you can understand. He gives you the *faith* you need to believe it and trust it, and He gives you the *power* to live it.

Those three amazing gifts come from the Holy Spirit, who loves you enough to take up residence in your mind and heart. Paul wrote in 1 Corinthians 6:19, **"Your body is a temple of the Holy Spirit within you, whom you have from God."** Here's more good news: the Spirit's presence in your life is a *gift* from God, and thus it is unconditional and free. You have a daily Companion and Counselor from heaven!

August 12

You Are Big Now

I'm not fond of windbags who are full of themselves. I love being with humble people—they seem more real and more approachable. They don't make me feel inferior. With them, I don't feel pressure to perform or pretend to be somebody I'm not.

But you know, there's also such a thing as false humility. Most of us are slick enough to feign ignorance or ineptitude when a job is coming that we don't like. Have you ever, like Jeremiah, tried to evade a grown-up role in God's kingdom work with the old modesty routine? **"'Ah, Lord God! Behold, I do not know how to speak, for I am only a youth.' But the Lord said to me, 'Do not say, "I am only a youth"; for to all to whom I send you, you shall go, and whatever I command you, you shall speak'"** (Jeremiah 1:6–7).

Thank God that Jesus didn't try to evade the tough job of the cross. He humbled Himself and became obedient to death so that we might have life and have it to the fullest.

Quit making excuses. Stop thinking of yourself as a spiritual child. Grow up. Get some training. Join us and be part of God's rescue team.

AUGUST 13

In View of God's Mercy

"Are you saved?" That old evangelistic question has been asked of millions of people. How are you saved? Jesus Christ lived, suffered, died on the cross, rose from the dead, and ascended for the very purpose of saving you. Who is saved? Those who believe it. Where does faith come from? From God's powerful means of grace: the Word, Baptism, the Supper.

Christians know what they're saved *from:* sin, death, and damnation in hell. Christians also need to know what they've been saved *for:* to serve God with their lives.

The Bible says in Romans 12:1, **"I appeal to you therefore, brothers, by the mercies of God, to present your bodies as a living sacrifice, holy and acceptable to God."** In other words, "God, You've been so good to me that my only possible response is to give myself back to You."

A living sacrifice is not a suicide bomber. It is someone who brings life to other people. How can God use you today?

August 14

Imitate Jesus

All of you know the taste of pain: your body, your dignity, your heart have all been hurt. And there's more pain to come in your future. All this is a result of sin, but it has become a part of God's loving plan. Our lives are designed to imitate Jesus Christ. His path to honor and glory led to a cross. Jesus now invites you to be like Him—to pick up your cross and follow Him.

How I resist that call, I'm ashamed to say. I wish Jesus had said, "If anyone would come after Me, let him pick up his cappuccino and follow Me." Or "pick up his martini and follow Me." Better yet, "get in his Corvette and follow Me."

The Bible says in 2 Timothy 2:11–12, **"If we have died with [Christ], we will also live with Him; if we endure, we will also reign with Him."**

This is the paradox: The harder we hang on to the things of this life, the more likely it is that we will lose them. The more we imitate Christ and deny ourselves, the more we will live.

August 15

We All Have Gifts

Parents can be cruel to children in many ways. Worse than physical abuse is crushing a child emotionally and psychologically. Imagine what it does to a small person's feeling of self-worth to hear "You're good for nothing."

Has anyone ever said that to you? Do you ever feel useless? God begs to differ. Nobody has everything, but nobody has nothing. We all have been given a surplus of some things that we are good at, in order to serve the gaps and needs in somebody else's life. And we've all been given the greatest gift—Jesus—whose gift inspires us to use our other gifts for Him and others. Peter wrote, **"As each has received a gift, use it to serve one another, as good stewards of God's varied grace"** (1 Peter 4:10).

Some gifts are obvious—great wealth, personal charm, great intellect. Other gifts are subtler but no less useful—patience with children, a sympathetic heart, a knack for speaking words of encouragement. How has God enabled you to make someone else's life better today?

August 16

We know we are uniquely made, but that doesn't mean we necessarily like it—right? Do you ever wish that you were not so different? If you're biracial, you might feel like you belong nowhere. People from both cultures make you feel like an outsider. Maybe God built you stocky, but you dream of being skinny. Maybe you're proud that you broke a gender barrier, but now you are the only female in an office of forty males.

But you know what? God loves diversity. If He fussed enough over creation to make every snowflake different, He certainly didn't want human communities of clones.

The beauty of this is that God builds unity out of the wild diversity of all believers on the planet. Galatians 3:28 says, **"There is neither Jew nor Greek, there is neither slave nor free, there is no male and female, for you are all one in Christ Jesus."** Nobody has greater value before God than anybody else.

There's a reason why you are designed the way you are and have been placed where you are. Ask for God's help to understand and appreciate the value of your own uniqueness.

AUGUST 17

God Controls Illness

What could be scarier than being sick—knowing that microscopic enemies of your health called viruses or bacteria have invaded you and are attacking your tissues? Medical science has made incredible progress in resisting disease, and yet, hospitals are still full, and people still pack clinic waiting rooms.

But get this: the God who made you is mightier than any disease that attacks you. It is a treat to read the stories of Jesus' healing miracles—fever, leprosy, and edema had to flee before His quiet and mighty word. **"When Jesus saw [the disabled man] lying there and knew that he had already been there a long time, He said to him, 'Do you want to be healed?'"** (John 5:6).

That same Jesus rules today, and He loves to act on behalf of His brothers and sisters.

He has lost nothing of His healing power, and He loves you as much as He loved the sick people He met. In your time of illness, find the sweet serenity of placing your life in His hands. He is still doing miracles.

God Sees and Remembers

Doesn't your heart break for the hamsters that run around in those little wire wheels? They motor as fast as their little legs can move, but they never get anywhere. I've never yet met a hamster who feels a great sense of personal accomplishment.

Are you a hamster? Or do you at least feel like one? Do your efforts go unrecognized, unappreciated, unnoticed? Do you run in circles? Do you toil in vain? Do other people always seem to get all the attention? Are you dying for somebody to clap and cheer for you just *once*? Do you know the sadness of feeling alone in a crowd?

Okay—stop right there. Recall for a second just who it is you're working for. Whose approval do you need first? Didn't I once hear you say that the Lord was the center of your life? Well then, here is His shout of approval for all those who humbly (and usually anonymously) serve others in His name: **"Well done, good and faithful servant. . . . As you did it to one of the least of these My brothers, you did it to Me"** (Matthew 25:21, 40).

Take this to the bank: God sees. God remembers. Your time will come.

August 19

It's All His

A bank teller looks at her cash drawer at the end of the day and says, "Mine." Foolish. A heavy-equipment operator plans on driving home in the road grader he's been in all day. "Mine," he says. Foolish. The youthful jewelry store clerk looks at the gems in the glass case and says, "Mine." Utterly foolish. They are laying claim to things that didn't originate with them and don't belong to them.

One of the reasons the theory of evolution is such a blight on Christianity is that it denies the Creator's work and ownership. King David laid out a beautiful, elegant truth: **"The earth is the Lord's and the fullness thereof"** (Psalm 24:1). Everything in the universe leaped into being at the sound and power of His creative word. Everything in the universe has a wonderful, loving purpose, and everything in the universe absolutely, positively belongs to God.

Thinking like this is learned behavior, and it has to be relearned on a regular basis. The Grand Canyon is His. The Rockies are His. The Great Lakes are His. The contents of my wallet, my checkbook, my portfolio, and my IRA belong to my God. And I get to enjoy them and use them for Him. It's all good.

Serenity and Confidence in God

If age only could; if youth only knew. There is a sweet trade-off, a sweet equilibrium to the way God designed human life. What older person has not intensely envied the young for their energy and strength? What older person has not felt a pang of sadness at the loss of his or her own youthful vitality? Have not the young always thought that since older people look saggier and talk slower, they must also be dumber?

Not at all. With gray hair and facial lines come knowledge and wisdom, the ability to know people and see trouble coming. With creaky knees come experience and knowledge about the way the world works. For those who have aged with the knowledge of their Savior, Jesus, age brings serenity and confidence that the Lord always keeps His promises and always rescues His people from their troubles.

With age comes the increased confidence that God's Word is true and reliable. Always true. Always reliable. When Proverbs 20:29 says, **"The glory of young men is their strength, but the splendor of old men is their gray hair,"** God is promising that grandparents will always have an important family role and never become obsolete.

Good Leaders Are Gifts

Good church leaders, like good parents, are a privilege not enjoyed by all. But if you live long enough, chances are very good that you will benefit greatly from some inspiring and passionate spiritual leaders.

Good leaders communicate well. They share passion, insights, and direction. They take care of the needs of longtime believers, and they reach out to the lost ones in society. They work like dogs, but they delegate cheerfully. They know how to say "Good job!" and "Thank you" and "It was my fault." They make following Christ look like the most wonderful thing in the world.

The Bible says, **"Remember your leaders, those who spoke to you the word of God. Consider the outcome of their way of life, and imitate their faith"** (Hebrews 13:7). Good leaders are gifts, not machines. Do you appreciate yours?

God in Love Designed You

Everybody, and I mean *everybody*, is looking for love. I've never met anybody who has had enough. We're all somewhat insecure about being loved. You know what's worse? Not knowing for sure if God loves you.

You can take great comfort in knowing that your life is not the result of some random string of evolutionary coincidences. The protein chains in you did not synthesize themselves. There is a cause behind your being. The Bible tells you that in love, God designed your very existence. Psalm 139:13–14 says, **"*You* formed my inward parts; *You* knitted me together in my mother's womb. I praise You, for I am fearfully and wonderfully made"** (italics added).

You are a masterpiece of human engineering. Look in a mirror and smile; looking back at you is proof that a divine Designer and Creator was in a good mood the day you rolled off the assembly line.

Husbands, Be Considerate

Here's another life puzzle: why do men generally have such a height, weight, and muscular advantage over women? In God's loving plan, His men have been given physical strength in order to provide stability and security so that everyone else can flourish.

Alas, some men take unfair advantage of their strength. God's Word challenges men to live in a better way: **"Husbands, live with your wives in an understanding way, showing honor to the woman as the weaker vessel"** (1 Peter 3:7). Good husbands listen—really *listen*—to their wives. Good husbands *notice* what their wives need. Good husbands don't compete and compare; they *complement.*

Christ, as our Bridegroom, was willing to die for His Bride, the Church. He noticed what we needed the most.

Good husbands respect the sacrifices their wives make. When women get married, they have to give up more than just their maiden names. The arrival of children crashes into the woman's life much more than into the man's. Guys, these sacrifices deserve our appreciation and respect. God made women different, not for us to feel superior, but to make our lives better.

All Have Sinned; All Are Justified

Everyone wants to feel good about himself or herself. Ah, but Satan, who is trying to destroy you, manipulates this desire and lies to you. He tries to flatter you that you are good enough for God just as you are. Since we are all so desperate to feel that we're okay, many of us fall for his line.

Here's the truth: the Bible says in Romans 3:10–12, "*None* is righteous, no, not one. . . . *No one* seeks for God. All have turned aside." Does that sound harsh and pessimistic? Well, it happens to be the truth.

But God has provided a way out. Here's more truth from His Word: though all have sinned, *all* are **"justified by [God's] grace as a gift, through the redemption that is in Christ Jesus"** (Romans 3:24). Absorb the full impact of that word *justified.* It means that God treats me "*just as if I'd* never sinned at all."

I hope you're smiling.

August 25

Gaze Upward

Have you ever been to Denver or talked with people who live there? If you have, you know why they moved there. In Denver, you never have to guess which direction is west. The foothills of the Rockies are like a towering western wall to the entire Front Range.

What is it about mountains that so rivets people's gaze? Psalm 121:1–2 says, **"I lift up my eyes to the hills. From where does my help come? My help comes from the Lord, who made heaven and earth."** Mountains act like a gigantic "up" arrow, lifting people's heads almost involuntarily. The mountains' rugged and wild beauty bears witness to the infinite power of God, who is older and bigger than they. The up arrow also points us to the One sitting at the right hand of God the Father. It's Jesus who personally invites us to come to Him when we are weary and burdened.

When all seems lost, when you are exhausted, when your labor seems in vain, find some mountains and look at them. Let them lead your gaze upward, away from your pain and troubles, up to the sky that is home to our friendly, sovereign God.

August 26

God Has a Purpose for Me

What could be worse than feeling useless? Everybody needs a sense of significance. Studies show that making a lot of money is not the prime motivator for people at work. Is it more vacation days? Nope. Of first importance is a feeling that what they are doing matters.

The apostle Paul wrote in 2 Timothy 1:9 that **"[God has] saved us and called us to a holy calling, not because of our works but because of His own purpose and grace."**

Are there days when you feel like just another wage slave? Do you have to drag yourself to work? Does your job leave you feeling exhausted and hollow?

Don't ever tell God that you are accomplishing nothing important with your life. He has you where He does for a reason. The influence you have on other people is often hidden from you. Someday He will let you see how He used you on His team.

The Lord Saves

What's in a name? How much can you tell about someone from his or her name? Well, you won't get much from mine. My first name means absolutely nothing. I guess my parents just liked the sound of it.

The names that God has chosen for Himself, however, have great meaning. Take the name *Jesus* for example. The Bible says in Matthew 1:21 that an angel came to a carpenter named Joseph to tell him that he would be the stepfather of the Savior of the world: **"You shall call His name Jesus, for He will save His people from their sins."**

The name *Jesus* literally means "the Lord saves." Think of it: your God came all the way to your world in order to take you to His world. Think of it: every time you praise Jesus' name, you are thanking God for your salvation. Think of it: every time you pray to Jesus, you are calling on a God who is kindly disposed toward you.

August 28

Heaven Is Worth the Wait

No one who has ever built a successful business has gotten everything right on the first try. Businesses that make money too easily at first tend not to listen to their customers very closely. Competition and struggle, setbacks and challenge all make businesses better, more efficient, and stronger *in the long run.*

When we don't get everything we think we want and need from God right away, this is not a sign that He doesn't care or that prayer doesn't work or that we are permanent losers. Sometimes God waits to give us things to make us tougher, more perceptive, more humble, or more patient. As we learn to live with some pain, we become more compassionate to people around us who live in pain.

The ultimate prize that God is preparing for you is so big, so good, and so easily lost by foolish sinners that He will put you through almost anything to make sure you make it. Here's His promise: **"Blessed is the man who remains steadfast under trial, for when he has stood the test he will receive the crown of life, which God has promised to those who love Him"** (James 1:12).

Hang on. It's worth the wait.

August 29

An Ambassador in Chains

Christians are taught to believe that God always takes care of His people. Does it bother you that believers seem to suffer so much? Is that a breakdown of God's promise of protective armor in your life? Is He asleep sometimes? on vacation? too bored or disgusted to bother with us anymore?

Paul wrote Ephesians 6:19–20 from a Roman jail: **"[Pray] also for me, that words may be given to me in opening my mouth boldly to proclaim the mystery of the gospel, for which I am an *ambassador in chains*"** (italics added). Here is yet another amazing example of how God operates—He turns even our disasters into blessings!

Since Paul could no longer move about freely as a missionary, God used him to become a missionary to the prison community. Since he could no longer move about freely, he had to train a group of younger men to take over for him. Since he could no longer travel, he needed to write letters to various individuals and churches, and we prize these epistles in our Bibles.

God may find your troubles particularly useful to His agenda. Don't curse your chains.

Use Your Tongue Wisely

The closer you live to other people, the easier it becomes to hurt them. You know how to push all your family members' buttons, don't you? We're all so insecure that we often resent a sibling's success. By nature, we assume that there is only one big piece of family-benefits pie, and that if one kid gets something nice, it automatically means a smaller slice for me.

You have the power to wound deeply. You also have the power to heal. Proverbs 12:18 reminds us, **"There is one whose rash words are like sword thrusts, but the tongue of the wise brings healing."** Many times, Jesus brought comfort and healing when He spoke such words: **"Your sins are forgiven"** (Luke 7:48). **"Father, forgive them, for they know not what they do"** (Luke 23:34).

Which issues are chafing the siblings in your family? Who gets to go to which school? Whose kids are the biggest overachievers? Who is doing what to care for elderly parents? True Christians cheerfully praise and encourage, trusting that God will meet their own emotional needs in His own sure way. Which wounded soul in your family needs your healing words today?

August 31

This Is Jesus' Dying and Living Gift

As I watched television accounts of the disastrous events of September 11, 2001, unfold in New York; Washington, D.C.; and Pennsylvania, I was awestruck by the numerous examples of brave citizens and rescue workers, some of whom literally lost their lives in the hopes of saving others.

In the collapse of those enormous buildings in New York City, some of the rescuers were so pulverized that their bodies were never found. Relatives of people who were safely evacuated from the Twin Towers will never forget New York's police and fire departments.

Shortly before He was arrested, tried, and killed, the Lord Jesus told His disciples, **"Greater love has no one than this, that someone lay down his life for his friends"** (John 15:13).

These examples from 9/11 remind us of an even greater display of self-sacrificing love: the work of Jesus the Savior, who was willing to lay down His perfect life so that dying people might live.

September

Ask, and it will be given to you; seek, and you will find; knock, and it will be opened to you.

Matthew 7:7

September 1

Let God Be God

I guess you know that each year, thousands of people hit such a level of frustration in their lives that they commit suicide. But that doesn't mean everybody else is happy. Henry David Thoreau wrote, "The mass of men lead lives of quiet desperation."

I think one of the greatest sources of frustration for us is our effort to control things that really are God's business. The Bible says in James 4:14–15, **"You do not know what tomorrow will bring. What is your life? For you are a mist that appears for a little time and then vanishes. Instead you ought to say, 'If the Lord wills, we will live and do this or that.'"**

Find the sweet serenity of letting God be God. He loves and accepts you. You can love and accept yourself. He forgives you, and so you can forgive yourself. He doesn't expect you to solve problems that don't belong to you. Love people and let them love you. And rejoice to find the little gifts God has given you along the way.

September 2

God's Goodness

Goodness is a funny word, isn't it? We use it all the time without really meaning it. "Oh, my goodness," we'll say. "Thank goodness." Think for a minute how much we depend on and luxuriate in the fact that our God is full of goodness.

Our frequently guilty consciences make us afraid that our first meeting with God will be dreadful because we think He will be so angry. Surely He must despise us because He is lofty and we are so low, because He is so pure and we are so polluted.

Here is one of Jesus Christ's main goals for His incarnation: to become an intensely personal message from the Father that God is good, that He really likes people, and that He is exerting huge resources to make our lives better. Look what Jesus did in the few short months He spent in public ministry: He eased people's pain, cured their diseases, rescued their children, and reversed their funerals.

King David wrote in Psalm 34:8, **"Taste and see that the Lord is good! Blessed is the man who takes refuge in Him!"** God is good all the time.

September 3

You Don't Have to Worry

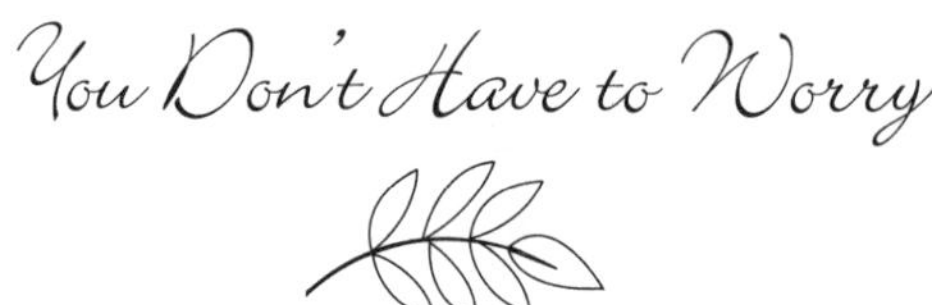

Tell me something—are you a worrier? Wait. Maybe a better question is, would the people who live with you call you a worrier? You know, it's one thing to be concerned, to plan, to think ahead. But worry is *fear,* plain and simple. It is fear that all your efforts to make your life better will be blown away by a hurricane of bad things.

Do worries keep you from falling asleep? make you blind to God's many blessings? make you irritable and depressed and crabby to the people around you? Does worry make you physically sick? Does it make your body physically ache?

The Lord Jesus speaks to your heart: **"Do not be anxious about your life, what you will eat or what you will drink, nor about your body, what you will put on. . . . Your heavenly Father knows that you need them all"** (Matthew 6:25, 32).

Take a deep breath and read that comforting verse out loud three times really slowly. The One who first said it means every word. He guaranteed it in the manger, on the cross, and as He ascended to heaven.

You can exhale now.

September 4

Honor Marriage

If you are old enough to remember President Kennedy, then you are old enough to have witnessed a transformation in American society: the change from general embarrassment and shame about "shacking up" to almost complete societal approval given to unmarried couples living together.

What do people give as a rationale? "We want to see if we're compatible." "We need to save money." "Since we will ultimately probably break up anyway, it will hurt less than an actual divorce." Older couples might say, "If we get married, one of us will lose some Social Security benefits."

God remains unconvinced. Actually, He is enraged by this casual trashing of His creation plan: **"Let marriage be held in honor among all, and let the marriage bed be undefiled, for God will judge the sexually immoral and adulterous"** (Hebrews 13:4). Find forgiveness in Jesus for all your rationalized arguments about shacking up. He can offer forgiveness because He took the judgment of God upon Himself.

Surely by now you have learned to trust God to tell you the truth—that His blessings will be upon people who honor marriage and keep their beds pure.

The Holy Spirit Intercedes for Me

There are times when everybody needs an advocate. Maybe you need somebody to speak for you when you don't know what to say, when you're too broken or weak to articulate things, or when you're in something way over your head. Maybe you get help from a coach, an attorney, or a parent.

Your ultimate advocate is the Holy Spirit. Who can bring your needs before the throne of God and speak on your behalf better than the Holy Spirit? The Bible says in Romans 8:26–27, **"The Spirit helps us in our weakness. For we do not know what to pray for as we ought, but the Spirit Himself intercedes for us . . . according to the will of God."**

Visualize it! Right now, the Spirit of the Lord is advocating for you! Nobody loves you more. Nobody cares more about your situation. Nobody can do more for you. You've got a Friend at the throne.

Use Alcohol Wisely

Do you drink? Do your friends? Did your parents? Have you had good or bad experiences with alcohol in your life? God created fermentation and distillation for people's benefit. The Lord Jesus not only attended a wedding where wine was being served, but He created another 120 gallons when the hosts ran out. He used wine as one of the two earthly elements in Holy Communion.

But like all of God's gifts, alcohol can be and is often abused. People in the ancient world (such as Noah) figured out how to get drunk not long after they discovered basic fermentation. God hates drunkenness: **"The works of the flesh are evident. . . . [They include] drunkenness. . . . I warn you, as I warned you before, that those who do such things will not inherit the kingdom of God"** (Galatians 5:19, 21). Alcohol abuse can destroy families, jobs, and physical bodies. It can destroy your soul too.

God has forgiven you through Jesus for your weaknesses and addictions. Be assured that He will help you resist temptation in the future.

Yet God chooses to treat you as a spiritual adult. He gives you a great deal of freedom in your choices. But you are not free to hurt your temple or hurt other people. Choose wisely.

I Can Overcome

I would love to look at my troubles as though I were in an airplane. At thirty-five thousand feet, even the mighty Rocky Mountains don't look so tough. Snow is pretty. Roaring rivers are just beautiful blue ribbons. The desert is simply a beautiful red-brown carpet.

Alas, in my life, I am not flying over my troubles. I bump into every one because I am not traveling through my life in a plane. I'm walking next to my oxen and my covered wagon. But here is God's promise to me (and to you): **"Call upon Me in the day of trouble; I will deliver you, and you shall glorify Me"** (Psalm 50:15).

Crossing the great American prairie was a lengthy ordeal, not a stroll. Your life is a long haul too, and God loves you so much that He allows hardships to toughen you for the trials of the journey. But you will make it because your God is with you. Call on Him. Expect deliverance. Honor Him when it comes.

God's Children Know How to Wait

"I want it, and I want it right now!" Four-year-olds talk like that. So do some teenagers, and so do childish grown-ups who have never learned to wait. One of the greatest life skills we need, to prosper both financially and eternally, is knowing how to sacrifice short-term pleasure for long-term gain. The harder parents are willing to work on this when their kids are little, the happier and more productive the kids will be as adults. Homework first, then play. Chores first, then toys.

The little schnauzer that was our childhood pet was a sweet pup, but we soon learned that we had better not touch her while she was eating. She would snarl and bare her fangs because from her canine point of view, that meal might be her last. One of the reasons why people are so impatient with their lives is that they are afraid there might be nothing good in their futures, so they had better get it now.

Psalm 27:14 says, **"Wait for the LORD; be strong, and let your heart take courage; wait for the LORD!"** In Christ the Lord, there are always good things in your tomorrow. Always.

September 9

God's Word Is True and Steady

We live in a world where everything is relative. Honesty can be bought and sold, morality is whatever the individual wants it to be, scientific truth lasts only until the next scholarly article, and personal loyalty evaporates like morning mist.

One of the things I love about God is that He has not left us to guess things such as who He is, what is right and wrong, and how we are supposed to act in order to have happy lives. There *are* absolutes in this relative world.

Psalm 119:89–90 says, **"Forever, O Lord, Your word is firmly fixed in the heavens. Your faithfulness endures to all generations."** Despite thousands of years of change and convulsion, God's true and steady words are here for you.

Wouldn't you like to pick up your Bible right now and listen to His voice?

Appreciate Diversity

The same Lord who made every snowflake in a blizzard different clearly enjoys that same diversity among the people He created. Yet the evil one has great success in using our human differences as wedges to drive us apart. Men and women clash; rich and poor fear and resent each other's behaviors; people who can't speak one another's languages can't understand and so don't listen; race and class provide endless opportunities for judgmental bigotry.

But you can shine like a star. **"Welcome one another as Christ has welcomed you, for the glory of God"** (Romans 15:7). If God cared enough to bridge the huge gap between His holiness and our lowliness, surely we can overcome gaps of mere gender, language, skin color, and income.

Christians have much to learn. After all, over the centuries, how many thousands of Christians, to the shame of the Church, were slaveholders or Nazis? What racism or resentments still lurk in your heart? Perhaps you have room to grow in the grace of acceptance.

September 11

Nothing Is Too Hard for God

Is it good to be skeptical? If you're a scientist, skepticism is considered a badge of honor. Scientists live to prove things. And it's by doubting, trying, and testing that the great principles and laws of the universe are uncovered and the properties of matter better understood.

Is it good to be doubtful and skeptical of God? Is it a good plan to devise tests to prove God's existence, love, wisdom, or power? Not such a good idea. Doubting God was the first human sin. In the string of things that Satan planted in the minds of Adam and Eve, the first step was to doubt God's Word.

Abraham's wife, Sarah, was in many ways the mother of all believers. But her bitterness at being childless was so great that she stopped believing that God had good things to give her or that a family could ever be hers. She simply couldn't believe that the child God had promised would ever come. The Lord said gently but reprovingly, **"Why did Sarah laugh . . . ? Is anything too hard for the Lord?"** (Genesis 18:13–14).

The Lord's words banish doubt. When your life shakes with doubt, listen to your God talking to you. Let His calm voice assure you that nothing is too hard for Him and that everything is going to be all right.

September 12

God Is Kind

Here's a question for you: do you love God? Hmmm. Did you say, "Sometimes"? It's kind of hard to love someone who you feel is judging you and condemning you, especially since we know we deserve His anger and punishment.

But guess what? The God who is holy is also the God who is *kind*. He commissioned His Son, Jesus, to rescue the world from hell and the grave. One of the Bible's favorite names for Jesus is *Messiah*. This name refers to the One who has been anointed, or commissioned, by God.

Meeting Jesus, the world's Savior, was a life-changing experience for a man named Andrew: **"He first found his own brother Simon and said to him, 'We have found the Messiah'"** (John 1:41).

Jesus is *your* Messiah. It was for just such a person as you and for just such a time as this that He suffered, died, and rose again from the dead. How can you not love someone who would do all that for you?

September 13

You Will Be Persecuted

Jesus' disciples were really looking forward to the visible reign of the Messiah, and they expected it at any minute. They were not into all the suffering talk, like taking up one's cross. They were much more into positioning themselves for cabinet positions in the new world order they felt sure was coming soon.

How disappointed they must have been to hear, **"Then they will deliver you up to tribulation and put you to death, and you will be hated by all nations for My name's sake"** (Matthew 24:9).

After Jesus' death and resurrection and after the Spirit's outpouring on Pentecost, they became fearless champions and confessors of the truth. They cheerfully trusted that Jesus could and would reimburse them later a hundred times over for any losses this side of the grave. That confidence sustained them during the bitter years of persecution.

Someday there will be only love. For now, there is plenty of hate, and some will come at you. Be aware.

God Listens

One of the most infuriating experiences known to man is trying to communicate something important to someone who isn't listening. "You're not listening to me!" is a complaint heard by millions of children from frustrated parents and by millions of husbands from frustrated wives. Behind that aching complaint is pure fear—fear that kids are going to ignore our advice, fear that our husbands won't take us seriously.

How terrifying, then, to fear that our prayers just clunk to the ground, unheard and unopened. What if God thinks that our needs and hopes and wishes are too trivial?

On the contrary! Jesus told believers how delighted God is to hear the prayers of His people and how eager He is to help them: **"Ask, and it will be given to you; seek, and you will find; knock, and it will be opened to you. For everyone who asks receives, and the one who seeks finds, and to the one who knocks it will be opened"** (Matthew 7:7–8). Could that be any clearer? Ask away!

September 15

He Gets Involved in My Life

Are you afraid of violence? When I was a kid, there were bullies on our playground, and once or twice, I was beaten up. Now that I've grown up and am 150 pounds heavier, it's a little harder to bully me physically. Yet I'm not so naïve to think that violence couldn't happen to me.

I'll tell you what, though: I am mighty glad that the Lord is not merely watching my life. He promises to get involved in my life—to protect me when I need it.

That promise is valid for you too. The poet Asaph wrote, **"At Your rebuke, O God of Jacob, both rider and horse lay stunned"** (Psalm 76:6). That goes for guns and knives too. When the God of Jacob raises His hand to shield His loved ones, nothing can hurt us.

He knows the date of my heavenly homecoming, and I am untouchable until that day comes.

Show Some Respect

Most people are desperate to feel big. We crave importance. We crave respect. That craving leads young men to join gangs, pack weapons, and pick fights. That craving leads young women to obsess over beauty and clothes.

Here is a better path toward self-respect: **"I say to everyone among you not to think of himself more highly than he ought"** (Romans 12:3). Here's another: **"In humility count others more significant than yourselves"** (Philippians 2:3).

Why is this so hard? It's because each of us struggles so much with self-hatred and depression that we can't give props to other people without seeming to make ourselves smaller by doing so. But listen to this: through our Savior, Jesus, God now looks at us with affection, approval, and admiration. Let those waves of mercy and goodness wash over you. Then let them flow from you to bless other people.

The more you respect other people, the bigger *you* will get. Think I'm kidding? Shock people and try it.

September 17

Money and Pressure

We all groan at the grotesque salaries that professional athletes and corporate heads pull down. We all know excess when we see it in others, in bloated signing bonuses and cushy stock options. But how about in your own life? How much money is enough? Let's be honest. Our usual answer is, "Just a little more—then I'll be okay."

You know the reality in our culture—America worships wealth. "If you've got it, flaunt it." But here's a quiet word from God: **"Some people, eager for money, have wandered from the faith and pierced themselves with many griefs"** (1 Timothy 6:10 NIV).

Do you think of your life and feel needy and deprived? How much pressure do you feel from neighbors and friends and relatives to show off your success (or hide your lack of success)? Does money make you somebody?

Let's get real for a minute. Think of how consistently the Lord has provided for you. How many days in your life have you gone without food? How many without clothes? How many have you gone without a person who loves you? Could it be that God is providing everything you really *need*?

September 18

God Is There for Us

We all expect to get sick now and then, and that doesn't bother us particularly. But when serious illness strikes, it can turn our lives upside down. Sickness shatters our illusion of control. Major sickness can destroy your savings. Your career. Your future.

God is there for us when we need Him. When we put our trust in Him, we give Him the chance to make the illness work for us. Once, when Jesus' friend Lazarus was seriously ill, everybody around him was panicking. But in John 11:4, Jesus simply said, **"This illness does not lead to death. It is for the glory of God, so that the Son of God may be glorified through it."** He then demonstrated His power by raising Lazarus from the dead and by raising up a strong faith in those who were there.

Even if you can't see it right away, God will make your life better in some significant way. Even more important, He uses major illness to advance *His* agenda. Your life becomes a canvas for Him to paint on. Your sickness will be for God's glory.

Christ Has Won God's Approval for You

Everybody needs approval from others. Even strong, self-confident achievers are hungry for approval. Think how your spirit has been crushed when someone you looked up to made some disparaging comment about something you did. You can probably still vividly remember putdowns that happened many years ago.

Our spirits long for God's approval even more. Do you think God likes you? If He were to comment on how you lived your life today, what would He say? Are you afraid of what He'd say?

Take heart. You can go about your life tomorrow knowing with certainty that God loves you, for His approval is based not on your performance but on Christ's. In Romans 5:8, the Bible says, **"God shows His love for us in that while we were still sinners, Christ died for us."**

That is the heart of the Gospel. God evaluates believers as though they were as wonderful as His Son. That's why He's smiling at you right now. That's why He approves of you.

September 20

I Need God

"Leave me alone. I can do this by myself." Parents are secretly glad to hear this from their kindergartners who proudly tie their shoelaces on their own. It is good to become independent.

But declaring independence from God is a whole other matter. Jesus once said that being cut off from God was as sure a path to death as when a branch is hacked off the central vine. Disconnected branches become dry, dead branches very quickly. So do disconnected people who die in their rebellion against God.

God loves us so much that He sometimes uses pain as a wake-up call to remind us of how much we need Him. God's agenda, God's strength, God's wisdom, and God's love all build us up to be bigger and better people than we could ever be without Him. Paul said, **"For the sake of Christ, then, I am content with weaknesses, insults, hardships, persecutions, and calamities. For when I am weak, then I am strong"** (2 Corinthians 12:10).

Here's a lovely irony: His power is made perfect in my weakness!

September 21

You can bear almost any burden if you think that tomorrow has a chance of getting better. If you're laid off from work or have a major chronic illness, you dream about the next interview, the next operation. But when hopes are crushed, the light goes out in your eyes.

The stories of God's Old Testament people Israel will break your heart. The years 721 BC and 586 BC mark the disintegration and collapse of the two kingdoms. But God told His suffering and exiled people, **"The days are coming, declares the Lord, when it shall no longer be said, 'As the Lord lives who brought up the people of Israel out of the land of Egypt,' but 'As the Lord lives who brought up the people of Israel out of the north country and out of all the countries where He had driven them.' For I will bring them back to their own land that I gave to their fathers"** (Jeremiah 16:14–15).

And He did! After seventy years of captivity, God restored the nation to its land, and at just the right time, He sent the Savior of the world to be born.

God knows your needs and your pain. You can give Him your fears. He had a plan for Israel, and He has a plan for you too.

September 22

God Watches Each of Us

Every boiler has a pressure gauge. That gauge is an extremely valuable indicator of the health of the system. The boiler engineer adjusts the pressure so it stays within the limits for which it was designed. He doesn't want it to blow open any joints or pipes on his watch.

When Christians suffer, and especially when they have it really bad, we're tempted to think that God isn't paying attention—or worse, that He doesn't care. Did you know that the opposite is true? Like a skilled boiler engineer, God watches each of us in our struggles, and He carefully sets limits to our pressures according to what He knows about our inner abilities.

The Bible says in 1 Corinthians 10:13, **"God is faithful, and He will not let you be tempted beyond your ability, but with the temptation He will also provide the way of escape, that you may be able to endure it."**

He made you. He loves you. He knows your capabilities.

September 23

True Sisters Grow Closer

It's hard to build things that last. Everything man-made is constantly eroding and cracking and crumbling. God intended sister-love to be lifelong, but like all good things, sister-love doesn't take care of itself.

Christian sisters grow in their relationship. They see things more clearly as time passes, they learn to let go of resentments, and they learn to cut their siblings some slack. They see that our patient God works it both ways—always making our lives better, sometimes through comforts and sometimes through hardships. Remember what Joseph told his once-cruel brothers? Genesis 50:20 records his kind and wise words: **"You meant evil against me, but God meant it for good."**

True sisters, tuned in to God's goals, are willing to let God draft them into His family rescue team. Just like Joseph, warmed by God's forgiveness for them, they look ahead optimistically, giving God's mercy a chance to work. And you know what they discover? Relationships based on mercy and faithful love really do last forever, and they just get better with time. Do you believe that?

September 24

A Sign of God's Love

What is more fragile and beautiful and fleeting than a rainbow? Untouchable, rainbows appear for a moment, shimmering wetly; and then they're gone. You can find various explanations for them in natural science textbooks, involving words like *diffraction* and *prism effect.* But God says that He makes them.

Noah's postflood world was very quiet and very empty. His future would be staggeringly difficult. But hey—he was alive! God told him and his boys, **"I have set My bow in the cloud, and it shall be a sign of the covenant between Me and the earth"** (Genesis 9:13). There would be no more universal catastrophes until Judgment Day.

From that day on, the rainbow has been witness to God's promise, patience, and mercy. Though the world richly deserves to be flooded again, God waits for people to come to their senses and return to His fatherly embrace. He wants you too, and it's not too late. Come home now!

September 25

Christ Clearly Revealed

Maybe it's just nostalgia, but doesn't it seem as though people years ago had a greater consensus on the difference between right and wrong? Today it is hard to know what is real, what is true. People grope for guidance, for something solid, something permanently true.

Far too many people today have bought into moral and spiritual relativism—that is, a worldview in which nothing is certain, nothing is absolutely true for everyone.

That's why Christians love God's Word so much, for it provides a rock of certainty for our lives. Paul once said to a group of Christians, **"Now I commend you to God and to the word of His grace, which is able to build you up and to give you the inheritance"** (Acts 20:32).

God's Word, the Bible, clearly reveals Christ our Savior. It gives you both the information you need and the power to believe it. It will build you up. It will make you sure of your heavenly inheritance.

September 26

Take Refuge in Him

We seem to be living in an age of rage. We have seen examples of road rage on the highways, air rage in crowded airplanes, and classroom rage in schools. People fight when they drink and fight when they fall out of love. Hatred among nations and peoples fills the earth with violence.

King David asks this question in Psalm 2:1: **"Why do the nations rage and the peoples plot in vain?"** It's bad enough that people fight with one another. Why would any sane person set himself against God and His wonderful plans to rescue a fallen world? Why would anyone see God's "claims on us" as "chains on us"?

We may never fully understand people's rage. But the Bible tells us what we *can* be sure of: the Father and His anointed Son rule over all things. **"Blessed are all who take refuge in Him"** (Psalm 2:12).

September 27

God's Love Letter

Does he love me?" "Does she love me?" The human heart longs for emotional security. We strain to look for signs in the words and actions of others to see what they really think of us.

To my amazement, my wife has kept all of my love letters to her. I guess that their words provide assurance to her, even though they were written decades ago. Here are words from one of God's love letters to His believers in the eighth century BC: **"'The mountains may depart and the hills be removed, but My steadfast love shall not depart from you, and My covenant of peace shall not be removed,' says the Lord, who has compassion on you"** (Isaiah 54:10).

Do you see where Isaiah is pointing you? Not at your flawed spiritual report card. Not at your cuteness or perfect performance of religious rituals or earnest promises. When you want to know if there's hope for you, be quiet and listen. Listen to God's love letter. Believe Him when He tells you that His love for you is His decision, that He will never fall out of love with you.

September 28

Reorder Your Priorities

Our U.S. currency contains some lovely wishful thinking. Right above the image of the Lincoln Memorial on the back of the $5 bill, for instance, is the legend "In God We Trust." I fear a more honest legend would be "In Cash We Trust."

Whatever you lean on, wherever you put your final trust—*that* is your god. Nothing but the true God in heaven can bear the full weight of your hopes, your needs, and your troubles. When you lean on something else, it breaks under the weight, and then you break too.

In what do you trust most of all? Is it your money? Is it your own wits? Moses was generally a pretty good example of a hero of faith. But occasionally even he slid into "In God we doubt" mode. In Numbers 11:23, the Lord overhauled and rebuilt Moses' faith: **"The Lord said to Moses, 'Is the Lord's hand shortened? Now you shall see whether My word will come true for you or not.'"**

The more you center your life, your hopes, your values, and your trust around the Lord, the stronger your life will be. Today would be a good day to reorder your priorities.

SEPTEMBER 29

Value God's Word

New employees in a marketing department don't start writing and selling their first day on the job. They must first spend some time learning about the company's products and services. They can't sell what they don't know.

If you are going to venture to speak for God, it is imperative that you know what you are talking about. The world has enough chatter about people's personal opinions, and nobody is likely to change his or her mind-set or lifestyle just because you say so. And so we drink deeply of God's words first for ourselves before we attempt to share this water of life with others. Psalm 119:16 says, **"I will delight in Your statutes; I will not forget Your word."**

Could you say that with a straight face? Or do you and your family need to get back into your Bible, learning the truths of Jesus' love contained there? Will you be in the Word today?

September 30

Help!

Has God ever kept you waiting for an answer to your prayers? Have you ever groaned with the prophet Habakkuk, **"O Lord, how long shall I cry for help, and You will not hear?"** (Habakkuk 1:2). God assured His impatient prophet that He was in complete control, that His solution to Habakkuk's problems would become visible at just the right time.

God made the ultimate statement by sending His Son, Jesus Christ, to a terrible death on a cross. By this priceless gift, He demonstrated how precious you are to Him.

Now He invites you to trust His love, His power, and His timing as He manages the world's affairs on your behalf. Psalm 30:5 says, **"Weeping may tarry for the night, but joy comes with the morning."**

OCTOBER

His mercies never come to an end;
they are new every morning;
great is your faithfulness.

Lamentations 3:22–23

October 1

Jesus Won; I Win Too

Every so often, public relations people do a poll on Americans' confidence about the future. They check on our level of optimism or pessimism about tomorrow to help investors and marketers decide on whether to advance or pull back.

You know, when people feel like there's no hope for them, they give up on all kinds of things—their friends, their families, their jobs, even their health. At times like that, it's great to hear how Jesus Christ has defeated all the enemies of the human race—sin, sickness, death, and hell. He told the believers in John 14:19, **"Because I live, you also will live."**

If our future is guaranteed (and it is!), we have incentive in the meantime to hang in there and hang on.

October 2

God's Sure Promises

Do you ever worry about your legacy? Will your children find stable careers? Will your children want to work in the family business? Can they take over for you? More important, will our present generation finally exhaust God's patience? Is He getting close to giving up on the human race? Will there be a future generation of Christians to keep the faith? Will the fire go out?

What a great time to listen again to the prophets. When the present looks shaky and you fear for the future of your family and community, how good it is to be reassured that your God is steady: **"I will pour My Spirit upon your offspring, and My blessing on your descendants"** (Isaiah 44:3).

The God who didn't give up on our parents' generation or ours has no intention of abandoning our children. Teach them. Trust Him.

October 3

Forgive

There must be something in estrogen that promotes development of human memory. Men would be sunk without their wives' formidable ability to remember birthdays, anniversaries, relatives' names, and children's clothing sizes.

The downside to that phenomenal memory is that women also tend to remember all too vividly the failings of their husbands and children. When those memories bring back pain, it gets harder to forgive.

We can't delete memories as if they were computer files. How can we forgive when we can't forget? Well, realize that anger never drains away by itself. We need to *choose* to get rid of it. God enables us to do just that! As we grow more aware of our sins and God's great mercy and forgiveness for *us,* we grow kinder toward those who have hurt us.

Paul has healing words for all who want to get rid of their grudges: **"Put on then, as God's chosen ones, holy and beloved, compassionate hearts, kindness, humility, meekness, and patience, bearing with one another and, if one has a complaint against another, forgiving each other; as the Lord has forgiven you, so you also must forgive"** (Colossians 3:12–13).

October 4

The Cross of Jesus Means Forgiveness

Why does God let bad things happen to good people? Are you ever troubled by this question? How can you reconcile your beliefs in God's great power and God's great love with the ugly reality of a world full of human misery?

It was not God who caused the world's misery. We did it. The Bible tells us that a compassionate God's great answer to the terrible problem of human suffering and human evil was to send His only Son—to suffer. On the cross of Jesus, the sins of the world were forgiven. Through His cross, Jesus opens up a beautiful new world where human suffering will be banished forever.

The Bible says, **"I consider that the sufferings of this present time are not worth comparing with the glory that is to be revealed to us"** (Romans 8:18). This is why God allows so much suffering in this world—so that we are excited to receive His gift of something better.

October 5

Our Dual Citizenship

The early Christians were often persecuted because their faith was viewed as a threat to the social and political stability of the Roman Empire. Nothing could've been further from the truth. Christians who shine like stars actually make the *best* citizens!

It is indeed true that we hold a dual citizenship, acknowledging the authority of both God and state. We live in two worlds: a sacred kingdom and secular kingdom. Can we do both? Absolutely! Peter (who would one day be martyred for his faith by the emperor Nero) wrote, **"Be subject for the Lord's sake to every human institution. . . . Honor everyone. Love the brotherhood. Fear God. Honor the emperor"** (1 Peter 2:13, 17).

All human governments, even bad ones, are actually God's agents of stability and order. How wonderful that we and our congregations don't just hunker down and hide in our holy fortresses until Judgment Day. How wonderful when we get out into our communities and help, clean, repair, and build. How wonderful when our acts of love and mercy, given as freely as Christ's love and mercy, touch and bless the lives of our neighbors, not just fellow church members. And how respectful when we refrain from ridiculing our elected officials, even when we strenuously disagree with them.

To love God is also to love your country, you know.

In Me You Have Peace

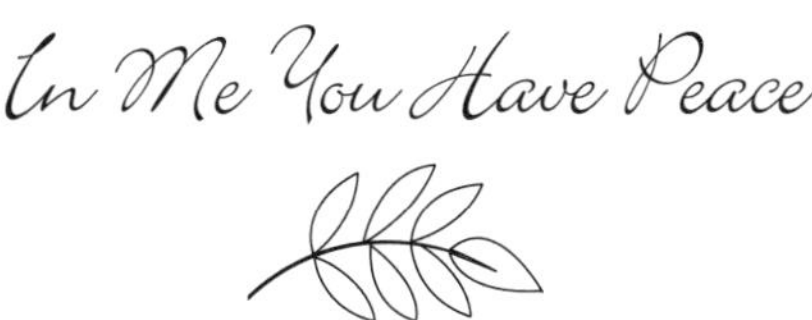

Does it look to you as though human civilization is unraveling? Many people are certain that the end of the world is near. Terrible diseases devastate entire continents. Natural disasters devastate communities, destroy homes and lives. Dreadful numbers of marriages come apart, permanently hurting everyone involved. Violent terrorist attacks break out all over the world.

Microdisasters also can grind down the human spirit: toiling in a dead-end job that just barely allows you to survive; working with mean and unappreciative people; living with chronic illness that leaves you exhausted every day.

Several hours before He won our salvation on the cross, Jesus predicted to His disciples that they and all believers would suffer much before coming into glory: **"I have said these things to you, that in Me you may have peace. In the world you will have tribulation. But take heart; I have overcome the world"** (John 16:33).

He won. We win.

October 7

We Will Be Safe

One thing that makes life miserable is being insecure. I don't mean just being insecure about how you look. I mean literally lacking safety—that you live in fear of being robbed, stalked, assaulted, molested, or raped, or that you live in fear that your children might be hurt. One of the best features of heaven is the absolute security that you will enjoy in your heavenly home. Completely safe. Joyfully safe. Forever safe.

The Bible says this about what God is getting ready in heaven: **"You prepare a table before me in the presence of my enemies . . . and I shall dwell in the house of the Lord forever"** (Psalm 23:5–6). In other words, in God's new world, we will never again know fear and insecurity, for all threats and all enemies will never again touch our lives.

Can you imagine what life will be like when you never have to be afraid again?

October 8

In 1945, after many decades of missionary work in China and with many churches staffed by expatriate missionaries from the West, there were still only about a million Christians there. Then came Mao and his Communist government that drove out or killed all missionaries and drove the Church underground.

Pure disaster? Not to the God who gets the last word. The Church grew far faster under persecution than before. Today there are tens of millions of Chinese Christians, and their churches are not dependent on the West.

Paul was an incurable optimist because he had seen so often how God could make trouble turn into progress. For instance, from prison in Rome, he wrote, **"I will rejoice, for I know that through your prayers and the help of the Spirit of Jesus Christ this [his imprisonment] will turn out for my deliverance"** (Philippians 1:18–19).

God has already seen your future, and it is a happy one. Go ahead—infect some gloomy person with your incurable optimism.

October 9

Secure in God Alone

Ever see children play the "trust" game? One kid will stand with his eyes closed and fall backward. Before he hits the ground, several other kids will catch him.

It is totally natural and understandable for people, including you and me, to find security in money. If we can just amass enough of it, we can rest easy. Our wealth will "catch" us when we fall. Proverbs 18:11 says, **"A rich man's wealth is his strong city, and like a high wall in his imagination."**

At best, that is a dangerously short-term strategy. Securities fraud, stock market collapse, theft, stupidity, natural disaster, and war can erode anyone's wealth, even that of kings. Your death will take it *all* away.

Want something much more secure that you can stake your life and your soul on? Paul was a secure and spiritually rich man, and he would love to share the wealth with you: **"The Lord will rescue me from every evil deed and bring me safely into His heavenly kingdom"** (2 Timothy 4:18).

From Every Nation, Tribe, and People

Without a doubt, racial hatred is one of the greatest problems that has ever plagued our country and our churches. Even today, after a brutal Civil War and a lengthy civil rights movement, we have achieved only an uneasy truce among the races, not true brotherhood and sisterhood.

Maybe this is as good as things will ever get in a sinful world. But God's vision is far brighter and warmer than mere *toleration* of one another. It is His goal to gather in heaven a multiracial, multilingual, multicultural family that will finally love one another as He loves them.

The Bible says, **"I looked, and behold, a great multitude that no one could number, from *every* nation, from all tribes and peoples and languages, [was] standing before the throne and before the Lamb"** (Revelation 7:9, italics added).

October 11

A New Life Without Sorrow or Death

What do you know for sure about what will happen to you when you die? The great British philosopher Bertrand Russell said, "When I die, I shall rot." Hmm. According to his worldview, you live a bit, and then—nothing.

The great Lord Jesus Christ, on the other hand, promised us a resurrection like His and a new life without sorrow or death. Faith in Christ connects you to the great Life Source who once created this world and can reenergize your dead body in the twinkling of an eye.

God's Word says, **"Set your hope fully on the grace that will be brought to you at the revelation of Jesus Christ"** (1 Peter 1:13). In other words, let your Savior and His powerful promises be your dearest treasure.

You interested? He gives it to all who trust and believe in Him. It is free, it is fun, and it is forever.

Heaven Is Forever

When jewelers advertise their merchandise, they love to boast about the durability of their gems. Unlike gifts of flowers or clothes, they say, diamonds are forever. Well, diamonds are indeed one of the hardest substances on the face of the earth. But even diamonds will disintegrate when Judgment Day comes and the whole universe is taken apart.

Do you want something that *will* last forever—I mean, *really* forever? The Lord Jesus promises that all who trust in Him as their Savior will have life—eternal life. And not just in spirit; our bodies will be immortal too.

Raised from the dead, transformed, and radiant in glory, we will not merely exist forever, but, as the Bible promises in Revelation 22:5, "**[we] will reign forever and ever.**" Now *that's* good news you can use!

October 13

Think of Others First

Every time I gas up my car, I get a little reminder of my sinful nature. Above the pumps, it says, "Self Serve." Boy, I love serving myself. I am endlessly fascinated by my own interests, appetites, and ideas. I love it when people do things for me. May I be frank? *My* agenda just seems so much more compelling than *yours*.

God's children, though, do a one-eighty. Jesus said that He Himself did not come to *be* served but to serve. Paul learned the joy of denying self and serving people, and he wrote, **"Do nothing from rivalry or conceit, but in humility count others more significant than yourselves"** (Philippians 2:3).

You can start by practicing on the people you live with. You can shine your faith by listening to their stories, sharing some of their pain, and looking for things to praise. And then God's magic kicks in—you start feeling better about yourself. The very best therapy for depression is to do things to make someone else's life better. Give it a try.

Living in Reality, Not Fantasy

It is not only men who indulge in risky or destructive fantasies. Women do too. Some women want a home and family so badly that they set up housekeeping with a guy and pretend to be married. They will put up with all kinds of abuse because as bad as it is, they fear being alone even more.

Some women cannot resist the fantasy that their love (or charm or determination) will "rescue" or domesticate a bad boy. To their great sadness, it turns out that bad boys generally don't want to be reformed.

Here is God's view: **"Do not be unequally yoked with unbelievers. For what partnership has righteousness with lawlessness?"** (2 Corinthians 6:14).

How can you tell if you are living a fantasy or living in reality? The reality is that your most important relationship is with the God who saved you. Don't put that at risk. Humble yourself. Listen to God. Listen to your family. Listen to your Christian friends.

October 15

"I Am Here"

Carole King once wrote a lovely poem about her dedication to a friend; no matter when, no matter where, no matter what season, she would be there as a good friend. Now, of course, Carole King isn't your friend, and she isn't going to be there for you, but I know Somebody who is, and who will be. His name is Jesus.

The King of kings and Lord of lords, the One who fills the universe, is interested in you. Yeah, *you.* Seriously! God is simultaneously far above you and also in the same room as you right now. He is both in heaven and in your heart. He speaks to you through His wonderful words in the Bible, and He hears absolutely everything you say to Him.

You don't need a cell phone or satellite radio to hear His wonderful voice: "You are not alone. It's okay. I'm listening. I'm here." **"I am with you always, to the end of the age"** (Matthew 28:20).

God's Grace Doesn't Wear Out

Doesn't it seem as if everything in your life wears out? Batteries lose their juice. Flowers wilt. Metal rusts. Clothes pill and tear. Even friendships fray and friends drift apart.

Everything wears out—except the wonderful grace of God. God is an absolutely inexhaustible source of strength for all who have put their trust in Him. Every day He has new gifts to give to believers: gifts of forgiveness, encouragement, and hope.

The Bible says in Lamentations 3:22–23, **"The steadfast love of the Lord never ceases; His mercies never come to an end; they are new every morning; great is Your faithfulness."**

Today there's a lot of talk about renewable energy resources—wind, hydroelectric, solar. Even they have limitations. The compassion and faithfulness of the Lord do not.

October 17

We Will Have Real Bodies

Everybody is curious as to what our bodies will be like in heaven. But I'll tell you what—you won't get accurate information from cartoons or TV shows or popular religious mythology. We aren't going to be transformed into angels—no wings and halos. We're not going to be spirits.

God has promised to raise us from the dead—soul *and body*. We will enjoy real, physical lives with God and with our fellow saints. Your legs were made for walking. Your arms will still embrace, and your face will still smile.

Thousands of years ago, a suffering but confident believer named Job said, **"After my skin has been thus destroyed, yet *in my flesh* I shall see God, whom . . . my eyes shall behold, and not another. My heart faints within me!"** (Job 19:26–27, italics added).

Mine too, Job.

October 18

Your Guilt Is Gone

Do you put off thinking about God because you are so ashamed of certain features of your life? Do you find it hard to pray because you'd feel like such a hypocrite? Have you sinned often, not out of ignorance but in spite of knowing better?

Are you possibly afraid of God Himself? Are you afraid that Judgment Day will be terrifying because you are so unworthy? Are you afraid to die? Well, guess what? Your Savior, Jesus, knew that you needed His help. He died and rose again to take away your guilt. All of it. He did it not to give a reward to the perfect but to be able to forgive sinful fools like you.

In repentance and faith, just throw your guilt at the foot of His cross. Jesus tells us that when the prodigal son returned home in sorrow, he humbled himself before his father. **"His father saw him and felt compassion, and ran and embraced him and kissed him"** (Luke 15:20).

That's the kind of hug from God that is waiting for you.

October 19

There Will Be Apostasy and False Prophets

It's bad enough that people have to suffer physically, but the evil one will also attack people's souls. He will make unbelief look attractive to some believers and persuade them to lose interest in the faith. All of us who love the Church, its worship and fellowship, its learning and outreach, want so badly to see steady, constant growth in numbers. We would like to think that someday, everybody will be converted to faith in Christ.

So would Jesus. But as He looked into the future, this is what He saw: **"Many will fall away and betray one another and hate one another. And many false prophets will arise and lead many astray"** (Matthew 24:10–11).

Faith in Christ keeps you mentally and spiritually healthy. If people throw away their faith, they get sick inside. Sick people hate and abuse others. Spiritually sick people will try to seduce others into their sickness, which of course leads to spiritual death. Now you know. Beware!

October 20

Think Ahead

Every parent knows how tough it is to persuade kids to think ahead. The default position of the human brain is to care only about *right now*. Think how compelling TV, YouTube, and video games are to people who should be doing algebra.

Satan thinks it's in his interest to keep your head down—to care only about your appetites and agenda *right now*. He uses dozens of addictions, distractions, and side-tracks to keep you from the truth.

The truth is that the future really matters. King Jesus is coming back with His holy angels to separate the believers from the unbelievers. Waiting until later to listen to God is flirting with spiritual suicide. Hebrews 12:2 says, **"[Look] to Jesus, the founder and perfecter of our faith."**

Right now is your personal time of grace to welcome God's good news.

October 21

He Always Has the Last Word

May I say that generally, I am not fond of my children having the last word? All too often, that last word is a complaint or criticism, usually accompanied by eye rolling, sighs, or *tsk*ing.

May I say also that I am ecstatic that my Savior always has the last word? Risen from the dead, ascended to heaven to the supreme seat of power over all things, the Lord Jesus has the final say over everything that happens on planet Earth.

Here are Scripture's promises to you: **"I am sure that neither death nor life, nor angels nor rulers, nor things present nor thing to come, nor powers, nor height nor depth, nor anything else in all creation, will be able to separate us from the love of God in Christ Jesus our Lord"** (Romans 8:38–39).

When Jesus has the last word in our troubles, it sounds like this: "I love you." "You will be okay." "I will guarantee that Satan can't harm you." "This is temporary—heaven is eternal." "Your fears are illusions—My commitment to you is real." "I will make even your hardships work out for your good."

Know what? I can exhale now. You can too.

October 22

Never Give Up

Allied resistance to the invading Nazi armies sweeping through Belgium had collapsed. In June 1940, it seemed as though all of Europe would fall. Winston Churchill had been Britain's prime minister for only a month, but he rallied the entire nation with his words to the House of Commons: "We shall fight on the beaches, . . . on the landing grounds, . . . in the fields and in streets, we shall fight in the hills; we shall never surrender." They didn't. The Allies prevailed.

Satan is a far more formidable adversary than even Hitler, but he can be beaten too. Never give up! Christ Jesus has crushed Satan's power over us and gives us the strength, through the Holy Spirit, to say no to his temptation to give up. No matter how great our losses, wounds, sins, and failures, all who hang on to Jesus in faith will ultimately inherit everything. James calls this splendid toughness *perseverance*: **"Blessed is the [one] who perseveres under trial, because when he has stood the test, he will receive the crown of life that God has promised to those who love Him"** (James 1:12 NIV).

Being a Christian doesn't mean that you never fall. It means that you never quit believing in Jesus.

October 23

Pass On Your Faith

Rebellion can hang on for a long time—even when young adults are having their own children. Christian grandparents can play a huge role in making sure that their grandchildren are baptized and hear the great news of God's love for them, especially when that middle generation is dropping the ball.

Scripture encourages older Christians to take great pains to pass on their faith to the younger ones: "We will . . . tell to the coming generation the glorious deeds of the Lord . . . that the next generation might know them, the children yet unborn, and arise and tell them to their children" (Psalm 78:4, 6).

Older people have learned by hard experience that Satan's promises are really painful lies. They have also come to appreciate God's "new every morning" forgiveness and the healthy life guidance from His Word.

Someday around God's throne in heaven there will be a meeting of all the saints who became believers in their Savior through the words, songs, and examples of their grandparents.

October 24

Finding the Balance

Christianity is serious business. It is about life and death—eternal life and eternal death. But living the Christian life is not all grim warfare, rigorous self-denial, and patient suffering. It is fun too.

Maintaining life balance also means creating space for downtime, for fooling around, having parties, relaxing, and enjoying God's beautiful creation. **"The disciples of John came to Him, saying, 'Why do we and the Pharisees fast, but Your disciples do not fast?' And Jesus said to them, 'Can the wedding guests mourn as long as the bridegroom is with them?'"** (Matthew 9:14–15).

Christ's work for us was completely successful, and that means that He has the last word. Since that last word is *forgiven*, the dominant emotion in our lives is joy.

Being an authentic Christian doesn't mean you have to pit Bible study versus athletics, church attendance versus family gatherings, prayer time versus camping. You can do all of these things. Find the balance.

October 25

Whoever Believes in Me Will Live

Even tough guys are afraid to die. In the weeks following the September 11, 2001, terrorist attacks on New York City and Washington, D.C., what became instant hot sellers? You got it—gas masks and vaccines. Terrorism does indeed breed terror.

We cling to life and do everything we can to preserve it. We pour billions into medical research and care. In the 1950s and 1960s, we built bomb shelters in case of nuclear attack. We work out, huffing and puffing on treadmills. We look for heart-healthy menu items. We eat vitamins and tofu, yogurt and bean curd.

And yet, no matter what we do, we will never be able to anticipate and defend ourselves and our loved ones against all the many ways that death could come upon us. There is only one way not to die—Jesus Christ. He alone holds the key to death. Jesus said, **"I am the resurrection and the life. Whoever believes in Me, though he die, yet shall he live"** (John 11:25).

If you just once allow yourself to believe that promise, all of your fear evaporates.

October 26

God Keeps His Promises

Have you ever really depended on somebody and then been let down? Did your dad promise a visit to the circus and it never happened? I bet you still remember your disappointment. Was there a man who promised to love you forever and have a family with you who lost interest and disappeared? It's human nature for people to fail, to lie, to quit, to make excuses, to be selfish, and to be so into their own lives that they don't have time for you.

One of the things I love about God is that He always keeps His promises. There is no evasion, no lying, no weakness, and no meanness in Him at all. He doesn't say it if He doesn't mean it and intend to follow through. What He says He will do, He does.

Kind David loved that about his God: **"Your steadfast love is great to the heavens, Your faithfulness to the clouds. Be exalted, O God, above the heavens! Let Your glory be over all the earth!"** (Psalm 57:10–11).

If He said it. That settles it.

OCTOBER 27

Remembering God's Promises

How is it possible that computers can store so much information on a hard drive? Even more remarkable, how is it possible that your brain can store as much information as the *Encyclopedia Britannica*, recalling smells from long ago, replaying complex music, hearing the voices of people long dead?

Memory is even better when faith in Christ lives there. Faith welcomes Christ's full and free forgiveness of our sins, and thus we can remember our own failings without guilt, self-hatred, or fear. A Hebrew poet named Asaph once wrote, **"I will remember the deeds of the LORD; yes, I will remember Your wonders of old"** (Psalm 77:11).

Memory also holds the promises of God as precious treasures. When we are old, when our limbs and fingers no longer move fast, it is a comfort indeed to call up God's track record of faithful love, forgiveness, and providing.

October 28

Pointing Out the Truth

Call me naïve, but there was a time when I didn't know what an intervention was. An intervention is a circle of friends who gang up on an alcoholic or drug abuser to tell him or her the truth, to break down the person's rationalizations and protective defenses, and to get the message through that he or she is on a path of self-destruction.

All of us—every man, woman, and child who ever lived—are "sinaholics," addicted to the lies and ways of Satan and hostile to God. Paul performed an intervention on one of the congregations he had helped to create: **"You were dead in the trespasses and sins . . . and were by nature children of [God's] wrath"** (Ephesians 2:1, 3).

This bad news has a good purpose. I can't love a Savior if I don't think I *need* a Savior. I can't believe in a Savior if I think I can tough it out by myself. I can't worship a Savior until I stop worshiping myself. Even though it hurts, we all need God's Word to tell us the truth about ourselves.

Hi. My name is Mark, and I'm a sinaholic.

October 29

God Controls Death

When you're making a list of the things that make the world look out of control, surely *death* will be near the top. What is more terrifying than seeing someone you love in a coffin or watching your own life slip away? Are you afraid of death?

In Luke 7:11–17, the Bible tells the story of how Jesus interrupted a funeral procession leaving the little town of Nain. First He told the sobbing mother, **"Do not weep"** (verse 13). Then He did something even more arresting: He raised the corpse of her son back to life.

It is Jesus' intention to give each of *you* that same gift—resurrection of your body and life forever with Him. Every coffin will be opened by our Lord—not in a ghoulish way as a grave robber, but as a grave liberator.

Have you ever noticed how funeral directors make the casket look like a comfy bed where the deceased is just taking a little nap? I kind of like it that way. When it's a Christian in there, that's what it is. Don't cry.

October 30

What is it about snakes that gives people the creeps? Is it their feel, their silent way of oozing and slithering around, or the terror of their venom?

A serpent was Satan's chosen vehicle for his deadly assault on the human race. Once a pure and glorious angel, Satan is now a fallen, hate-filled, wretched spirit. He struck back at God by attacking God's children. But that attack was a sneak attack. Satan did his damage by planting doubt, lies, fear, and ego in the hearts of God's two children.

You know Satan's voice because you have felt thoughts and impulses like the one that seduced Eve: **"The serpent said to the woman, 'You will not surely die'"** (Genesis 3:4). He lied. Human rebellion against a holy God brought the triple curse: human pain, certain death, and eternity in hell.

Don't baby yourself. Go through your life with eyes wide open. You have a fearsome enemy who is coming at you like a snake—quiet, hate-filled, patient, deadly, serious. But know this also: your Savior has crushed his head.

October 31

In the Direct Presence of God

If you listen for it, you will hear the word *heavenly* pop up in people's talk now and then. "Heavenly" desserts and chocolate treats, Caribbean cruises, and therapeutic massages are all nice. Unfortunately, the things we call "heavenly" on earth are pale shadows of the grand reality.

In heaven your pain will be gone. You will get back all the Christian friends and loved ones that you laid to rest. You will live in absolute security, bothered no longer by Satan and his temptations. You will never sin again.

But the best is that you will be very, very close to—actually in the personal presence of—our God. You will be very close to the ultimate Source of life, goodness, and love, and you will feel it throughout your being.

In Revelation 21:3, John writes, **"I heard a loud voice from the throne saying, 'Behold, the dwelling place of God is with [people]. He will dwell with them, and they will be His people, and God Himself will be with them as their God.'"**

NOVEMBER

From His fullness we have all received, grace upon grace.

John 1:16

Jesus Was Punished for Us

Everything you have ever learned about proper justice teaches that those in authority should punish the guilty and release the innocent. We hate hearing stories about people wrongly imprisoned, and we hate it even more when an obviously guilty criminal gets to walk.

Yet that's exactly what God did to rescue you. Nobody would have guessed this marvelous secret if God hadn't revealed it because it seems to make no sense. But it's the truth, and it's your only chance. In God's court, the innocent God-man, Jesus Christ, was convicted and executed. The obviously guilty parties—you and I—are pardoned unconditionally. No, really. Seriously.

Nobody ever expressed this unexpected and shocking good news better than the prophet Isaiah: **"Upon Him was the chastisement that brought us peace, and with His stripes we are healed. . . . The Lord has laid on Him the iniquity of us all"** (Isaiah 53:5–6). Have you found the utter peace of mind and soul that comes from letting go of your fear of God's punishment? Jesus did it all for you. You are free to go.

Pray in the Spirit

Talk is cheap, we say. Words seem weak compared to knives and guns. Yet words addressed to an almighty God through faith in Christ access that almighty power. The Father loves to hear from His children, and He intervenes in our lives to shield us from Satan and his evil ones.

Does it surprise you that Paul lists prayer with the other armor and weapons in Ephesians 6? **"Put on the whole armor of God,"** he says in verse 11, **"praying at all times in the Spirit, with all prayer and supplication"** (verse 18).

Think of it—the Lord of the universe actually invites you to direct His formidable power to do things that make your life better. He must really think that the content of your prayers is important. He must really like you.

NOVEMBER 3

Cradled in God's Hands

Are you a "tough guy" who's not afraid of anything? Or are you a "nervous Nellie" with so many fears that you don't know where to start to list them? Fear holds us back from trusting and believing. Fear paralyzes. Fear makes our painful memories much more intense. Fear makes us blind to the blessings we have, and fear makes it difficult, even impossible, to believe that there will be good things to come.

God's Old Testament people, the nation of Israel, had much to worry about in the eighth century BC. Their armies were being battered, their cities looted, and their cattle stolen. People were being captured and enslaved. Their nation was being nibbled away, leaving a smaller and smaller core of what once had been a mighty empire.

In those bleak times, Isaiah had some wonderful words to tell God's people. They could trust and believe in a God who was not going to let them lose their true treasure. In fact, God would actually be using the hard things in their lives to help them! God said, **"Fear not, for I am with you; be not dismayed, for I am your God; I will strengthen you, I will help you, I will uphold you with My righteous right hand"** (Isaiah 41:10).

When you find yourself being afraid, take a deep breath, listen to these words of God, and remember that you are being cradled in God's very big hands. You are safe.

November 4

Caring for Your Spouse

Becoming a believer in Christ is the most profound change that can happen to a person. Marriage is the second. Marriage changes *me* to *we*. Marriage makes two people one flesh. Marriage forms a new organism, and the husband and wife are now of the same tissue. Their nervous systems are now connected. When one is miserable, the other groans. When one is happy, the other smiles.

Happy is the couple who recognizes their interdependence. Men generally take longer to figure this out. Here's some help, guys, from Paul: **"The husband is the head of the wife even as Christ is the head of the church. . . . Husbands should love their wives as their own bodies. . . . For no one ever hated his own flesh, but nourishes and cherishes it, just as Christ does the church"** (Ephesians 5:23, 28–29).

Did you follow that? Headship in a home is not primarily about issuing orders or exercising power. It is about taking the lead in taking care of the other people in the home. It is being as energetic in seeing to the needs of the others as you are about pampering yourself.

God designed marriage so that when husbands take care of their wives, their own lives get really good. Guys, what does your wife need from you today?

NOVEMBER 5

God Does Not Change

Sociologists tell us that all change brings stress. They tell us that we can take on only one major change a year without serious emotional trouble. Some of these major changes include getting married, suffering a serious injury or illness, changing jobs, moving, and becoming parents.

Imagine how stressed out we would be if God were constantly changing on us. One of God's characteristics that we don't prize highly enough is His steadfastness.

James 1:17 says that "**[God] does not change like shifting shadows**" (NIV). His love for us is eternal, His purposes are rock solid, His Spirit is steady, and His commandments are timeless. He has never lied to us, has never gone back on a promise, and will never give up on us.

November 6

Moms, Share Your Faith

When the cameras close in on professional athletes, they never say, "Hi, Dad," do they? It's always, "Hi, *Mom*."

It's not that dads are unimportant. But in their moment of triumph, people go with their gut. They just blurt out the first emotional thing that occurs to them. And when they want to share joy and give credit, where do their hearts go? To Mom.

Moms, what does that tell you about the value of sharing your faith in Christ with your kids? God is entrusting these dear ones into your care, and He is assuming, expecting, *demanding* that you lead them to Him.

God had Moses lay these instructions on all of His people shortly before Moses' death: **"These words that I command you today shall be on your heart. You shall teach them diligently to your children, and shall talk of them when you sit in your house, and when you walk by the way, and when you lie down, and when you rise"** (Deuteronomy 6:6–7).

Don't you love being a Christian? Isn't it great knowing that God loves you, forgives you, works in you, blesses you, and will raise you to eternal life? Do your kids believe that?

November 7

What God Has Done

All the King's horses and all the King's men couldn't put Humpty together again.

Kings' horses and kings' men can't put the broken world back together again either. The best and brightest brains in human history have struggled with devising ways to get God (or the gods) to like us again, and what have they come up with? Witch doctors. Voodoo. Chanting, dancing, and meditation. Human sacrifice.

God's wonderful Word tells us what we could never have figured out by ourselves. This is the core of His love letter to humanity: **"In Christ God was reconciling the world to Himself, not counting [people's] trespasses against them"** (2 Corinthians 5:19).

Jesus Christ accomplished something even tougher than reassembling a huge broken egg-man. By reliving everyone's life and dying everyone's death, Jesus brought people back into God's presence—His friendly presence. We are reconciled!

November 8

God Controls the Demons

Here's a question for you: What thing most threatens your world? Who is your worst enemy? Is it an angry and bitter family member? your boss? your debt load? a serial killer? suicide bombers?

Actually, your worst nightmare comes from hell itself. Satan and the demons that live there, sad to say, have access to our world and are working to cause you pain and destroy you. But the Lord Jesus showed during His ministry that even hell's demons have to obey Him. The Bible promises that when Jesus returns, He will throw Satan himself into everlasting damnation: **"The devil who had deceived them [will be] thrown into the lake of fire and sulfur"** (Revelation 20:10).

Do you see how this changes everything in the way you look at the future? Your worst enemy has already been defeated. He is precondemned, his power broken, and he cannot take from you your most valuable possessions.

November 9

Make the Most of Opportunities

Do you ever hear yourself saying, "I'll be happy when . . . " or, "I'd be happy if . . . "? How green does the grass look on the other side of your fence? Is happiness something external that comes to you? Is personal fulfillment always right over the next hill? Do you get depressed waiting for your life to get better?

Paul wrote in Ephesians 5:15–16, **"Look carefully then how you walk, not as unwise but as wise, making the best use of the time, because the days are evil."** Every day brings God's gift of opportunity for service, growth, and change. Every day the Lord will bring before you what He needs you to do for Him, and that humble service brings satisfaction to your heart that will last.

Happiness is portable. It is also contagious. And we have the most contagious happiness of all because our happiness flows out of Jesus' love for us. You know what? Today has been a great day, and tomorrow is going to be even better.

NOVEMBER 10

God Forgives and Forgets

You know all about the grudging way we mortals "forgive" one another. "I'll forgive, but I can't forget." Since we can't forget, ugly memories keep coming back and draining off our willingness to forgive.

Ready for yet another Gospel surprise? Here is an amazing prophecy and promise from Jeremiah, a humble minister of God who had to watch the Babylonian captivity take place before his own eyes. Here is God speaking to sinful Israel (and speaking also to you): **"I will forgive their iniquity, and I will remember their sin no more"** (Jeremiah 31:34).

Here's another puzzle for you. Is God absentminded? Does He have heavenly Alzheimer's disease? If God is omniscient, how could He lose track of data like this? The answer is that God *chooses* not to remember our failures (a feat we're not capable of). Because He looks at us through the lens of the cross, He can indeed forgive *and* forget.

Do you know what that means? You can live each moment of each day without dreading that the hammer will fall.

Confusion During Times of Loss

Ever been blindsided by a personal disaster? Sometimes trouble brews slowly, and you can see it coming. But other times, the blow falls without any warning—you are given a cancer diagnosis, or a tragic car accident leaves you or a loved one disabled. The loss is bad enough. What makes it worse is the fog of confusion. A sudden loss can really disrupt your peace of mind. Why didn't God stop this from happening?

God is not only in control of the universe in general, but He is closely monitoring your life in particular. He takes inventory of every hair on your head. He further promises to make absolutely every one of your life experiences—the joyful ones and the miserable ones—work for you.

Here's an unshakable rock you can stand on, written by a man who experienced plenty of hardships: **"We know that for those who love God all things work together for good, for those who are called according to His purpose"** (Romans 8:28). Did you get that? At this very moment, God is working for your good.

November 12

God's Children Are Obedient

Do you like to be told what to do? No? Well, to be honest, I don't either. Inside our brain is a mulish arrogance, a perverse stubbornness to do everything our way. I am intensely interested in my own comfort and preferences. Yours don't interest me particularly.

Tell you what—adults who act like that are unemployable. You can't hold a job if you aren't willing to serve someone else's needs and let someone else tell you what to do.

This is why parents have such a crucial responsibility to teach their children to obey. You can reason with the kids later. You can discuss things with them later. Job 1 is obedience. If children can't learn to obey their parents, they will never learn to obey God, and that means spiritual death. In Isaiah 1:2, God laments the disobedience of His people: **"Children have I reared and brought up, but they have rebelled against Me."**

There is a better way. Colossians 3:20 simply says, **"Children, obey your parents in everything, for this pleases the Lord."** Our desire to obey our parents doesn't occur because of a threat or a feeling of obligation. Rather, it's out of gratitude for Jesus and the blessings of forgiveness and life He gained for us when He obeyed the will of His Father. Which way of life appeals more to you? Which way do you think God will bless?

November 13

I Can Relax

Around the time of the First World War, automobile trips were an ordeal. Roads were unpaved and had to be shared with livestock. Cars were fragile and often broke down. Tires blew out constantly. Service stations were few and far between.

Today I never think twice about jumping into my car and driving long distances. I enjoy many advantages that my grandfathers did not: smooth interstate highways, steel-belted radial tires, air bags, well-engineered vehicles, cell phones, and AAA motor club service.

My God is even better than AAA. **"Whoever confesses that Jesus is the Son of God, God abides in him, and he in God. So we have come to know and to believe the love that God has for us"** (1 John 4:15–16). He keeps me running, provides me with maps, jump-starts me when my battery is low, tows me when I break down, provides fuel along the way, and even lets me steer.

I can relax and enjoy the journey of my life knowing that my God is committed to getting me to my destination.

November 14

Appreciate Your Teachers

Let's face it: the Bible is a big, intimidating book containing years of history, descriptions of ancient cultures far different from our own, the names of obscure people and places, and the mysteries of God's identity and works.

What a joy it is to learn from experienced teachers! From nursery school moms to Vacation Bible School volunteers, from Sunday School staff to parish school educators, from youth ministers to pastors and professors, God has lavishly given great people to share His great message. The Bible says that it was *God* who **"gave the apostles, the prophets, the evangelists, the shepherds and teachers, to equip the saints for the work of ministry, for building up the body of Christ, until we all attain to the unity of the faith"** (Ephesians 4:11–13).

Nobody has to start from scratch. We all benefit from the huge boost we get from our Bible teachers. Who taught you God's Word? Was it several people? You owe God several thanks. Remember your teachers. Love your teachers.

November 15

God Loves Human Sexuality? Really?

The Christian community in the early centuries struggled to maintain a balanced view of human sexuality. The missionary hero Paul was single and urged others to imitate him. The words *virgin* and *Mary* became welded together and seemed to indicate that God had a strong preference for perpetual virginity. Jesus Himself never married. And so some concluded that human sexuality is essentially dirty and impure, a gross necessary evil for the propagation of our species.

Does it surprise you to know that God delights in human sexuality and approves of it? Think about it—He invented maleness and femaleness. He was so excited about His first two people that He didn't let them live singly. He brought Eve to Adam in marriage immediately upon her creation.

Without a doubt the least-read book of the Bible is the Song of Solomon. People don't know what to make of it. It sounds like the libretto for a musical about a passionate romance. Actually, that is exactly what it is, and it demonstrates how God designed sexual attraction in marriage for our joy.

***"He[:]* Behold, you are beautiful, my love; behold, you are beautiful; your eyes are doves. *She[:]* Behold, you are beautiful, my beloved, truly delightful. Our couch is green"** (Song of Solomon 1:15–16).

November 16

Value All Life

In spite of all the progress the United States has made in according civil rights to all people, there is still a dreadful bias against those with a "diminished" quality of life. Sonograms now help mothers detect and abort unborn children who are projected to have disabilities. When the newborn son of columnist George Will was found to have Down syndrome, a hospital staffer asked him and his wife if they intended to take the baby home. In shock, they could only mumble that they thought that's what parents generally did.

Here is King David's view of the high value that God places on all human life: **"You formed my inward parts; You knitted me together in my mother's womb. I praise You, for I am fearfully and wonderfully made"** (Psalm 139:13–14).

Your witness can speak for the speechless. Your words can give value to people considered disposable. Remember that God wants all people to enjoy life with Him. He's commissioned us to tell the whole world about Him. Remember that in heaven, these disabled folks will be your equals in every way through Christ. What will they say to you when you meet them there?

November 17

Our God Is Big

All of us struggle to control the uncontrollable. We try to control other people, control the weather, control growth, control time, and stop the aging process. When those efforts fail (as they always do), we get frustrated. We feel small, weak, and insignificant.

But you know, feeling small is not such a bad thing. Consider the relentless changing of seasons. Without you lifting a finger, the physical climate all around you continues in a steady pattern of regular change.

That restless cycle of sun, wind, falling leaves, ice, mud, and buds is designed, set in motion, and sustained by the gentle, omnipotent hands of God. He likes a change of scenery, and He thinks you will too. God told Noah, **"While the earth remains, seedtime and harvest, cold and heat, summer and winter, day and night, shall not cease"** (Genesis 8:22).

The annual cycle of our seasons is a silent reminder of God's infinite power, His creative genius, and His faithful promises. What a comfort it is to enjoy being very small and watching the world whirl around us.

He Gives Me the Faith I Need

By now you know that God is a judge and that He will evaluate every human being who has ever lived. He holds the world accountable for all thoughts, words, and deeds.

But God is no ordinary judge. A judge at a track meet would be disqualified for cheating if he helped a long jumper avoid scratching or grabbed the pole vaulter's pole so it wouldn't knock down the bar.

Here's what I love about God: He not only came personally to our planet to rescue us. He conquered sin, Satan, death, and hell for us and gives eternal life to us by faith in the Savior. But it's even better than that: He even gives us the faith we need to believe the message and be saved. Whoa—that's seriously good news, folks.

We absolutely must have His help to jump-start our dead hearts. Scripture says, **"No one can say 'Jesus is Lord' except in the Holy Spirit"** (1 Corinthians 12:3).

He Inspired the Holy Scriptures

When people are skeptical about some information or a command that's laid on them, they protest, "Who says?" All of us absolutely *hate* being pushed around. We want to know the authority behind the command.

All of us are awash in religious claims and pronouncements from people claiming to speak for God. How can you ever know for sure what to believe?

The Bible says that **"all Scripture is breathed out by God"** (2 Timothy 3:16); it also tells us, **"Men spoke from God as they were carried along by the Holy Spirit"** (2 Peter 1:21). In other words, God the Holy Spirit has made it His personal mission to use human writers to get His divine ideas down on paper. He has controlled the process so thoroughly that to read the Bible is actually to hear the voice of God Himself.

All Scripture is God-breathed. That means that you don't have to pick your way through the Bible, trying to guess which verses are God's. They're all His.

Rely on Your God

"Every day, in every way, I'm getting better and better." Steady repetition of this phrase is how French psychologist Émile Coué taught people at his clinic in Nancy to will themselves into a better future. This type of autosuggestion came to be called Couéism and found many followers.

People want badly to believe that the world is steadily evolving into a higher state. Science-fiction novels and movies sometimes portray ideal societies where people have progressed beyond the need for violence and war.

It is a wonderful thing to be self-sufficient and to work at bettering yourself. It is a terrible thing, though, to suppose that we don't need God. We are not evolving into better people. If anything, people are slowly devolving into beasts.

There's a better way. **"Trust in the Lord with all your heart, and do not lean on your own understanding"** is the wise counsel from Proverbs 3:5. Every day, in every way, we are loved and blessed by our dear Father, Savior, and Counselor.

November 21

You Need Your Family

Among the cruelest and stupidest words known to man are the words *I don't need you.* These have been flung at family members by disgruntled spouses and angry kids. Nothing could be more wrong.

You only get one set of birth relationships. Our identities and securities are wrapped up with these sometimes-nice, sometimes-foolish folks. Whenever we cut these ties, something dies inside us. Conversely, the more we tend these relationships and the better we take care of them, the happier and more fulfilled our lives will be.

An amazing widow named Ruth came to realize not just how much her widowed mother-in-law, Naomi, needed her, but how much Ruth herself was depending on Naomi. The dear older woman was ready to set the younger woman free of any sense of obligation, but Ruth wouldn't hear of it. **"Where you go I will go. . . . May the Lord do so to me and more also if anything but death parts me from you"** (Ruth 1:16–17).

Can you get the words "I need you" past your teeth today?

Model Jesus' Love

People use the word *love* all the time. Generally, they mean that they respond favorably to things and people who are lovable. People love flowers, chocolate, sports, and cars. People love other people when they are nice or good-looking.

Jesus' love is different. Jesus loves the unworthy, the dirty, the broken, the failures. Jesus didn't "fall" in love with us. He *chose* to love us. His love is unconditional, universal, and free. His love is not a reward for our worth. His love *gives* us worth.

He invites—commands—His sisters and brothers to reflect and radiate that kind of love out into our loveless world. **"Love one another with brotherly affection. Outdo one another in showing honor"** (Romans 12:10). Jesus' sad prophecy was that over time, the love of most would grow cold. What an absolutely marvelous way for you to bear witness—to love as He loves.

Look around you. Who needs your love today?

November 23

Jesus Has Removed Your Sin

Everybody feels guilt. Do you like it? Of course you don't. Guilt is horrible. It is a dead weight on your soul. It cloaks your view of the future with dread. It creates shame.

And yet, guilt is good. God put consciences inside us to tell us when we do wrong. Our guilty consciences make us aware of our need for Jesus' forgiveness. In grateful humility, we stretch out our hands and receive mercy.

Satan can't stand for us to be at peace, so he tells us that we're not really forgiven. He tells us that we're too evil, that we don't deserve mercy, that we've sinned too often. But those whispers are lies.

Here's the truth: **"As high as the heavens are above the earth, so great is His steadfast love toward those who fear Him; as far as the east is from the west, so far does He remove our transgressions from us"** (Psalm 103:11–12).

When your conscience is troubled, don't look at yourself. Look at Jesus and exhale.

November 24

Live Like Travelers

Do you possess your possessions, or do your possessions possess you? The only reason I've stopped acquiring more stuff is that my house is already overfull. Think how many people have to park in their driveways because their garages are packed full of other stuff.

Some people have lives uncluttered by possessions because they are poor. Poverty does bring some spiritual advantages, doesn't it? It's much harder, isn't it, to travel light when you have much? Peter calls us **"aliens and strangers in the world"** (1 Peter 2:11 NIV). How can you live like that when your life is so loaded down with stuff?

Here is some wisdom from Paul: **"We look not to the things that are seen but to the things that are unseen. For the things that are seen are transient, but the things that are unseen are eternal"** (2 Corinthians 4:18). Having stuff is not evil in and of itself. These are the real questions: Where is your heart? What do you value most in life? Since we must leave behind absolutely every material possession, let's keep looking up and traveling light.

November 25

God's Fingerprints

"I knew it! I always pick the slowest line!" "I'm always the last chosen." "If only I were making just a hundred dollars more! I can't ever seem to get a break."

Ever catch yourself indulging in that kind of self-pitying, bitter talk? Satan is trying to poison your mind by suggesting to you that you're on your own, that nothing ever goes right, and that you are destined to be a loser. He wants you to feel cheated, to be convinced that God is disengaged from your life.

In fact, if you take a careful look around, you will see that your life has been filled with blessings from God. Blessings are God's interventions in your life to make it better. Your friends, education, government, rainfall, food, and family are all gifts. They are signs that God loves you!

What is the antidote for self-pity and bitterness? How about Paul's prescription: **"Rejoice always, pray without ceasing, give thanks in all circumstances; for this is the will of God in Christ Jesus for you"** (1 Thessalonians 5:16–18).

Being thankful is figuring out cause and effect in your life. Look at your happy moments and notice more and more the fingerprints of God all over them.

November 26

A Spouse Is a Precious Gift

It is amazing how quickly the joy and tenderness of newlyweds can morph into irritability and withdrawal. Can discontented wives learn from the painful sighs of widows? Can disappointed husbands learn from Proverbs 18:22: **"He who finds a wife finds a good thing and obtains favor from the Lord"**?

It is *good* to be married. A decent husband provides strength and security so that his wife's creativity and emotion can soar. A decent wife provides respect so that her husband will know that there is always one place for sure where he is treated like a man.

"It is not good that the man should be alone," God said in Genesis 2:18. The single life has adventure and independence, as Paul showed us. But a dear spouse is a sign of God's favor, a precious gift uniquely good. Imagine the possibilities when a husband and wife see each other as individuals made holy through the perfect life and sacrificial death of Jesus. Imagine the possibilities if husbands and wives would treat each other as precious gifts from God.

How Good He Has Been to Us

A woman once complained bitterly about her husband's snoring. Her friend, a widow, said, "I would give anything to hear my husband snore again."

In our better moments, we look around and are ashamed of our complaining. We see God's fingerprints all over our lives—in our families, places of work, communities, and churches. We enjoy daily bread, roofs over our heads, and free forgiveness of our many sins. How good He has been to us!

The apostle John wrote, **"From His fullness we have all received, grace upon grace"** (John 1:16).

When was the last time you said, "I love my life"? Have you ever said, "I am rich"? Who last heard you say, "I am blessed by the best"?

The Love of Most Will Grow Cold

Is the quality of life improving year by year in our country? To be sure, some things are better. There is much less blatant racism in the United States now than there was when I was a boy.

But our cities are now far more violent places. Marriages are far more fragile, and many couples never bother to get married in the first place. Out-of-wedlock births are out of control. Girls who should be playing with dolls are pregnant. Pornography accounts for a preposterous percentage of Internet traffic. Children are neglected and abused, robbed of their childhood, and forced to deal with adult issues.

Every year, unscrupulous chemists devise new illegal drugs that promise more-intense highs and deliver more enslavement into depression and addiction. Increasing wealth turns many into self-absorbed pigs. With all of our advanced technology and growing wealth, how can these things be happening? Why can't people evolve along with technology?

Jesus wants you to be realistic: **"Because lawlessness will be increased, the love of many will grow cold"** (Matthew 24:12). Now is a great time to share God's idea of improvement for the world—faith and trust in the promises of God through Jesus' love. Now you know.

November 29

Blessed Are the Poor?

When you read the Gospels, it certainly seems that Jesus is pretty hard on wealthy people and kind to the poor. He said that it was easier to get a camel through the eye of a needle than to get a rich man into heaven. He even told a rich young man to give away all of his money. Is poverty God's preferred state of existence? Does money corrode our values so badly that we are best rid of it? Is the vow of poverty that monks and nuns take God's ideal way of life?

Didn't Jesus talk about poverty in one of the Beatitudes from the Sermon on the Mount? Actually, yes. **"Blessed are the poor in spirit, for theirs is the kingdom of heaven"** (Matthew 5:3). But note that the poverty Jesus praises is not financial but spiritual. To be poor in spirit in this verse means to be humble, to be aware of our sinful need for a Savior, to be aware that without Jesus' help, our hands are empty in the judge's court.

You can have a hefty income and still be appropriately poor in spirit if your heart is humble and grateful before your God, if your greatest treasure is found in the Gospel of Christ, and if pleasing God is the chief goal of your life.

November 30

A Western tough guy explained to a padre why he didn't pray much: "Prayin' is beggin'. I don't beg nobody fer nuthin'." This hombre took self-reliance to a sad extreme. In fact, prayer is not beggary. Human dads love to hear from their children, and they love to help children in their time of need. How much more does our great heavenly Father absolutely love the intimate spiritual communication that He invented, blesses, and guarantees?

Here is the concept: the Master of the universe invites all believers to send messages to the throne via their Savior, Jesus. He promises to answer all requests in the way that will do us the most good. He is loaded with good things to give us and is intentionally just waiting to be asked. What do you need right now?

Here are Paul's wonderful words of encouragement for you: **"Do not be anxious about anything, but in everything by prayer and supplication with thanksgiving let your requests be made known to God"** (Philippians 4:6). Note to self: This ain't beggin'. This is respondin' to my Daddy's sweet invitation.

DECEMBER

Sing to Him, sing praises to Him;
tell of all His wondrous works!

Psalm 105:2

December 1

People hope for all kinds of things—championships for their favorite sports teams, a huge lottery win, a big promotion, great weather, and rising stock prices. Sometimes those things happen. Often they do not. Our hoping for them does nothing to make them happen.

God invites His all-star team to be hopeful. That doesn't mean to wish on a star. It means to be utterly convinced that our future will be better than the past. It means that we can be optimists, since God lives in our future already and is making things better for us *right now.*

Here's His promise to you: **"Many are the afflictions of the righteous, but the Lord delivers him out of them all"** (Psalm 34:19). Here's the beauty of it: It's not our doing. It's God's. We can bear anything because we know everything in our lives will get better in the future. We hope that. We know that.

December 2

Co-workers

St. Paul never heard of the festival of Kwanzaa, but he would have liked at least one of the seven principles, *Ujima* (collective work and responsibility). He wrote, **"Greet those workers in the Lord, Tryphaena and Tryphosa. Greet the beloved Persis, who has worked hard in the Lord"** (Romans 16:12). Those women, and the cheerful attitude they brought, made Paul's ministry-organizational chores a lot lighter. He loved his work. He loved even more working *with them.*

It's a special blessing to be able to work with people who share a common faith in Jesus. That shared bond of faith impacts positively how we think of others and how we work with them.

Look around you at your place of work. Perhaps you will see people who complain, gossip, or steal. But you may also see people who remember your birthday, know the names of your kids, and call when you're sick. There is a special bond between people who work hard on a successful project. Are there some nice people on your team? Thank You, Lord!

December 3

Did God Make Me Gay?

One feature of life in the twenty-first century is that living the gay lifestyle has come out of the closet. Now that TV shows celebrate gay life and legitimize gay and lesbian heroes, it must be okay, right? Homophobia is added to the list of universally condemned cultural sins, along with anti-Semitism and racial prejudice.

One of the most powerful arguments made by gay apologists who still try to be Christian is that "God made me this way." It seems undeniable that some people do indeed have a natural inclination (that is, a weakness) for such feelings and activities. But that does not make it right, any more than the fact that some people seem unusually susceptible to alcoholism, violence, or lying and conclude that God made them that way.

Here is what God thinks about a homosexual lifestyle: **"Men likewise gave up natural relations with women and were consumed with passion for one another, men committing shameless acts with men and receiving in themselves the due penalty for their error"** (Romans 1:27).

We do our gay friends no kindness by helping them justify sin. True love seeks to help people who struggle in this way to get help in redirecting their emotional desires or at least to trust God enough to live a life of chastity.

God Holds No Grudges

How many people do you suppose are angry with you right now? I try to live in peace with people as best as I can. But I'd guess there are probably at least a half dozen people who would like to hurt me if they could.

What a relief it is to know that God holds no grudges toward me, even though I deserve His anger. In the Bible, the prophet Jeremiah said, **"The steadfast love of the LORD never ceases; His mercies never come to an end; they are new every morning"** (Lamentations 3:22–23).

Aren't you glad that you're forgiven through Jesus? Aren't you glad that God does not keep records of your wrongdoings? Aren't you glad that you can start out each day anew, celebrating the Lord's compassion instead of being afraid of Him? Life with God is good!

December 5

Live Like Servants

Are you into pampering when it's *you* who's getting pampered? Do you like manicures, pedicures, massages, saunas, whirlpools, and room service with chocolates on your pillow? Who doesn't love being waited on and fussed over?

It's one thing to enjoy occasional treats. It's another when people adopt a life attitude that sees other people only in terms of what they can do for *me*. The sin within each of us makes us full of ourselves, makes us users of others instead of lovers of others.

The Lord Jesus Himself calls you to reevaluate your self-image. He invites you to enjoy seeing yourself as a servant (like Him) and to enjoy making other people's lives better. Only hours before He died, He laid some "servant therapy" on His disciples: **"If I then, your Lord and Teacher, have washed your feet, you also ought to wash one another's feet. For I have given you an example, that you also should do just as I have done to you"** (John 13:14–15).

Serving others is God's way for your life. It is the way of true worship, authentic joy, and personal satisfaction. Remember the King's highest praise on Judgment Day? Is it "Well done, mighty, wealthy prince"? Nope. "Well done, good and faithful servant."

December 6

Have you ever wanted something important but realized that you could not afford it? What was it that you wanted—a new bike? a motorcycle? a Caribbean vacation? admission to that elite university?

Let us talk about the ultimate wish. Are you interested in going to heaven when you die? You might think that God would demand a huge payment or sacrifice before He would let you in. You might think that you had to perform valiant service, go on a dangerous quest, slay a dragon, or prove yourself to be a hero in some other way. But guess what? He simply gives it away to all who believe in Jesus as their Savior.

He says, **"Come, everyone who thirsts, come to the waters; and he who has no money, come, buy and eat! . . . Incline your ear, and come to Me; hear, that your soul may live"** (Isaiah 55:1, 3). This is God's wonderful grace—and it's free!

December 7

He Loves You

"All You Need Is Love" was a hit anthem for the Beatles in 1967. It's kind of a hippie cliché, isn't it? And yet it's true. We are all hungry, even starving, for love. We all need to be validated, to be of value to somebody. How could we trust in a God whom we fear or who seems to despise us?

But here's what's really going on: in His personal love letter to the human race, which we call the Bible, God sets us free from the terrible pressure of self-justification. He went first. **"This is love: not that we loved God, but that He loved us and sent His Son as an atoning sacrifice for our sins"** (1 John 4:10 NIV).

This is love: to be willing to go first to restore a relationship. This is love: to inconvenience yourself to bring good things to someone else. This is love: to show kindness and mercy to someone smaller and lowlier than you. This is love: to see worth even in someone who is bad. God is love. All you need is God.

December 8

Marriages Belong to God

There is nothing particularly sacred or holy about business contracts. When they are no longer benefiting you, you can terminate them as you please. Don't like that lease? Don't renew it.

People who look at marriage like a lease can't possibly build one to last. When you are always looking at an open door behind you, you lack motivation to work through the challenges that come upon sinful people in a sinful world, and you will then miss out on the satisfaction and bonding that come from mutually conquered problems.

People who look at marriage the way they look at their business contracts imagine that they are the owners. God begs to differ. As the inventor of marriage and as the inventor of humanity itself, He dares to claim our marriages as His own. Seriously! Jesus said, **"What therefore God has joined together, let not man separate"** (Matthew 19:6).

God would like you to see your marriage as a beautiful, valuable possession that belongs to Him, like a priceless porcelain vase, but that He willingly lets you hold and enjoy. If you drop it, you are not only losing out yourself, but you are smashing something that God thinks is His.

December 9

We Love to Worship

Can you imagine a packed home crowd watching its team win the NBA championship in game seven and sitting quietly when the final buzzer sounds? Do you think even one person in the arena would be indifferent? bored? lethargic? Not a chance!

Everything good in our lives can be traced directly or indirectly back to the triune God. Flaming sunsets, summer rain, grand canyons, majestic mountains—all are from Him! Our amazing human bodies, families and friends, constantly replenished food supply—all are from Him! Our spiritual rescue on Calvary; our triumph over sin, death, hell, and Satan; the everlasting home waiting for us—all are from Him! Let me hear you! Are you ready for some worship?

Make some noise! **"Oh give thanks to the Lord; call upon His name; make known His deeds among the peoples! Sing to Him, sing praises to Him; tell of all His wondrous works!"** (Psalm 105:1–2).

December 10

Is Your Gift Serving?

Have you ever noticed how God's kingdom runs on principles that are opposites of the principles of our sinful world? For instance, God says, "The last will be first," and, "Whoever wishes to be great must make himself like a child." TV shows lavish attention on the rich and powerful. God prizes humble service.

The Bible says, **"We have different gifts, according to the grace given us. . . . If [someone's gift] is serving, let him serve"** (Romans 12:6–7 NIV).

Do you know people like that? Just think about how our lives are enriched by people who prepare meals, clean up after others, plan events, and send greeting cards. Just think about the many people who get their first look at real Christianity by watching a Christian cheerfully give of himself or herself to make somebody else's life better.

Can you say "It makes me happy to make you happy"?

December 11

A Second Time Around

Isn't it fun to see older adults get giddy about becoming grandparents? What is it about another generation of messy, needy babies that gets them so excited? And what is it about grandparents that makes grandkids appreciate them so much?

Maybe it's because people who were aware of their own faults as parents are grateful to God to have another shot at helping to raise children. Maybe it's because maturity brings serenity. When you're more secure in your own identity as a forgiven child of God, you can be much more patient with the faults of others. Maybe it's because life has taught them that loving people is more important than acquiring stuff. Just ponder for a moment Jesus' love for us.

Proverbs 17:6 celebrates that special magic which jumps generations: **"Grandchildren are the crown of the aged."** Seniors, wear your crowns with pride! Your time and unconditional love are very special gifts that your grandkids need—and will *never* forget.

Your Body Is God's Workmanship

One of the annual rites of spring all around the United States is clusters of schoolchildren trooping through zoos and museums on field trips. There they will find "helpful" information about the origin of the universe and of mankind itself. They will learn about billions of years of evolutionary development, the Paleozoic Age, and Cro-Magnon man in the natural-history displays.

What they will *not* hear is anything about creative design, about a guiding mind and power that put the universe together. In museums and zoos, all the beauty and complexity of animal and human life is assumed to be coincidental and spontaneous, undesigned and meaningless.

David, king and poet of Israel, had better information: **"*You* formed my inward parts; *You* knitted me together in my mother's womb. I praise You, for I am fearfully and wonderfully made"** (Psalm 139:13–14, italics added). Know what? You are not the result of a coincidental string of unexplainable protein self-syntheses. You, too, are a product of God's knitting works. God knew you, chose you, and had a plan to bring you into His family of faith before you were even born. Your entire body is a walking showpiece of God's brilliant design, engineering, and craftsmanship. Be proud of your body. Honor Him with it.

December 13

You Wear the Uniform

It's not just sports teams that love to wear their colors. Sports fans, bridesmaids, restaurant wait staff, and jockeys all proudly wear uniforms that identify them with their team.

The day that you were baptized, you were given the uniform of heaven to wear. You might call them the "colors of Christ." The Bible says in Galatians 3:27, **"For as many of you as were baptized into Christ have put on Christ."** You can't see these clothes (yet). But what matters most is that God can.

He sees the clothes of Christ and claims you as He does His Son. He sees the holiness of Christ wrapped around you and regards you now as holy as His Son. The angels have absolutely no trouble picking out which are God's own. They shine.

December 14

He Talks to You

Can you imagine trying to assemble an automobile without an instruction manual? Absurd. Impossible. Can you imagine trying to figure out the meaning of the universe and the meaning of you without blueprints from God? Absurd. Impossible.

One of God's most precious gifts to you, a gift that shows how highly He values you, is His Word, the Bible. He wants you to know what He's like, what He's done, how He thinks, how He talks. Paul praised the Christians in Thessalonica because in hearing Paul's proclamation of the Word, they recognized that they were hearing the voice of God Himself: **"When you received the word of God, which you heard from us, you accepted it not as the word of men but as what it really is, the word of God, which is at work in you believers"** (1 Thessalonians 2:13).

It is a sign of how dear you are to God that He took such elaborate pains to prepare a document that explains everything you need to know about life on earth and life in heaven. And guess what? It's now available in English! All you have to do is read it.

Serve One Another

The great English poet John Donne once wrote, "No man is an island, entire of itself." The God who created us would most heartily agree. It was His wonderful plan to give spiritual gifts to each believer with the idea that we would use these gifts to help and serve one another.

The Bible says in Romans 12:4–5, **"For as in one body we have many members, and the members do not all have the same function, so we, though many, are one body in Christ, and individually members one of another."**

Here is one of the delightful secrets of God's ways: you will find your greatest fulfillment and satisfaction in life when your agenda involves interacting with and taking care of other people. If you want to test the validity of that statement, why don't you just try it for a week?

December 16

The Day Will Burn

Did you believe in Santa Claus when you were a kid? I imagine most people did. Santa stories can be imaginative fun for little children. That is, unless people actually start to believe the "Santa Claus Is Coming to Town" malarkey.

It's bad enough if children believe that their gifts really came from a fat guy in a red suit. What is far worse is if this seemingly omnipotent and all-seeing elf becomes people's pattern for how God operates. After all the hype and threats and bluster, even naughty boys get nice presents, not coal, in their stockings. I fear that many reasonably intelligent people suspect that God can see everything, but that there will be no consequences for sin. Just as Santa claims to see who's been naughty or nice *but then gives presents to everybody anyway,* they think God will ignore our naughtiness, and everybody will get some pie by and by.

Wrong. God's righteous judgment over sin will slam into the planet. The prophet Malachi wrote, **"Behold, the day is coming, burning like an oven, when all the arrogant and all evildoers will be stubble. The day that is coming shall set them ablaze, says the Lord of hosts"** (Malachi 4:1).

It is a healthy and sane response to tremble before the righteous anger of a holy God. A day of wrath is coming. Now you know.

December 17

We Are Forgiving

Why is it so hard to forgive other people? There are many compelling explanations. Here's one. As any accountant could tell you, a debt owed to you is a type of asset. If you are holding a debt that someone else owes you, you have moral leverage over that person. You can feel superior, nobler, better than that person. If you give it away for nothing, you could feel as though you just squandered an asset.

How pathetic our grudges must seem to the One whose boundless mercy forgave a world of sinners. The chasm He bridged to reconnect the holy God with sinful people like us is far greater than any gap between people. Christian behavior looks like this: **"Forgive us our debts, as we also have forgiven our debtors"** (Matthew 6:12).

There's a treat for you here. Forgiving other people not only shows obedience to a direct command of God. It also frees you from the prisons and poisons of your own anger.

He Gives Me the Holy Spirit

One of today's popular phrases goes something like this: "I'm not religious, but I'm spiritual." By this, people seem to mean that they are vaguely aware that there is more to life than making babies, making money, and making a name for themselves. Alas, those same people are pretty vague about what that spirit is or where it comes from.

Here's the real spirit we need to be truly spiritual: the Holy Spirit, Person number 3 in the Holy Trinity. Through the Word of God and through Baptism (which is Word + water), God the Holy Spirit actually comes to live within a person. Paul wrote to a young pastor: **"He saved us . . . by the washing of regeneration and renewal of the Holy Spirit, whom He poured out on us richly through Jesus Christ our Savior"** (Titus 3:5–6).

You are not alone as you fight Satan. You are not powerless against the demons outside and inside. You are not clueless about life's great questions. Know why? Because you are Holy Spiritual.

Faith During Times of Loss

We all enjoy fantasizing about quick solutions to our troubles—a big lottery hit, miraculous pills to fix medical problems, a beautiful new car dropped off at the curb, a jackpot from the slots or roulette wheel.

You and I both know that those things rarely happen and that we'd be fools to count on them. I'm not going to lie to you—it can be hard to keep believing in God's beautiful promises when the outward outlook of our lives often seems so grim.

Though we see the damage he has done, we can't actually see Satan and his demons at work. But neither can we see the disasters that didn't happen because of God's many interventions. When we pray about being broke, God's answer might be to prevent our car from breaking down. Or maybe there was going to be a fire in your house, but He prevented it from starting. Though we can't see God's holy angels, we can trust that they are on duty and flawlessly executing God's orders for our protection. Hasn't God already delivered us from the greatest disaster—eternal separation from Him? Yes! He will certainly be with us during the tough times in our lives.

Here is a faith-building promise from your Father: **"Are they not all ministering spirits sent out to serve for the sake of those who are to inherit salvation?"** (Hebrews 1:14).

Give It to God

Everybody gets stressed—debt, grades, layoffs, family arguments, crime. Everybody suffers loss—friends, income, health, even hope itself. Think of somebody in your home. How does that person get rid of stress? How do *you* deal with stress?

You're a sinner, so you have probably developed some pretty hurtful ways to blow off steam. Do you yell? blame other people? get quietly depressed and beat yourself up? get bitter? get drunk? find various ways to run away?

All of these sad coping mechanisms assume that you're all alone—that nobody cares and nobody is there to help you. I know Somebody who always cares, who is always there for you. **"Cast your burden on the Lord, and He will sustain you; He will never permit the righteous to be moved"** (Psalm 55:22). He's big enough to take it. He's loving enough to welcome it. In fact, He already solved the problem of your sin for you.

What is upsetting you right now? Visualize putting all of that stress into a gunnysack. Now throw it on God. Right now. I mean it—yes, you. Do it right now.

Model Trust in the Lord

One of the most miserable pieces of baggage that many of us drag around is the feeling of anxiety. Some men worry. Most of the women I know worry a lot.

That constant, chronic fear can leach into your children's attitudes like contaminations seeping into your drinking water. Kids need their parents to model trust and confidence in the Lord. Parents, when you are in prayer with your Lord, present not only your fears and needs, but reflect also on all the things that God has helped you overcome in your past.

It takes no genius to count your problems. Counting *blessings* is learned behavior, and the more you notice God's work in your life, the less anxious you will feel. Paul has wonderful words to lift up your heart right now: **"The Lord will rescue me from every evil deed and bring me safely into His heavenly kingdom"** (2 Timothy 4:18).

You know, things will work out. God loves you, and He loves your kids too. You're going to be okay.

December 22

Share Your Faith

You've said it a hundred times—a thousand times: "Hallowed be Your name." Let's encourage one another to mean it. The ultimate light shining from Jesus' all-star team, the most joyous reason to have your name inlaid in the heavenly walk of fame, is not only your own belief in Jesus Christ, but your willingness to share the message so clearly and warmly that another lost soul, precious to the Savior, comes to faith as well.

God doesn't expect you to be able to preach like Peter or pray like Paul. But He does expect you to use the gifts that you have been given and to make use of the opportunities He sends. **"Always [be] prepared to make a defense to anyone who asks you for a reason for the hope that is in you; yet do it with gentleness and respect"** (1 Peter 3:15).

Sharing your faith doesn't mean long and clever arguments, loads of "proof passages," or following some complicated methodology. Just listen to people's stories and resonate with their fears and pain. Just tell the stories of what Jesus did for the world. Just tell the stories of what Jesus has done for you. Just say, "Come with me. There's room for you. You'll like it here. Jesus is the *best!*"

December 23

I Can Surrender

Do you work out? Do you use old-fashioned, he-man free weights, or do you use those new-fangled, electronic "progressive resistance" machines? Either way, the concept is the same—without resistance, without a load, you cannot grow stronger. Without resistance, you might as well just sit in a chair and slowly get fatter.

This explains why your life is often so hard. Those hardships are not because God doesn't love you anymore or because He's losing His grip on reality or has lost track of your issues. He *allows* them in your life to provide resistance. God does His best work in your life in times of crisis. That's how He changes you and grows you.

"Why are you cast down, O my soul, and why are you in turmoil within me? Hope in God; for I shall again praise Him, my salvation and my God" (Psalm 43:5).

Don't argue with me. Right now, take a deep breath and say these words: "Lord, You have brought me to faith and have promised to send Your Holy Spirit to keep me in the faith through Your Word and Sacraments. Starting today, I promise to see my struggles and hardships as opportunities for Your work and my growth. Make me stronger! Increase my faith!"

Close to Heaven

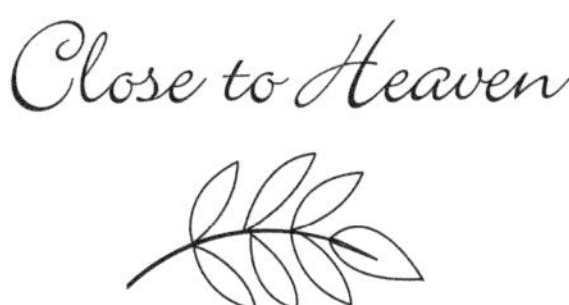

When I was a little kid, in mid-December, my folks would close off the doors to the living room where the Christmas tree was. We could peek, but we weren't allowed in there until Christmas Eve. You can only imagine the tension we felt.

Do you dread getting old? Yeah, I know—some things *are* hard. The loss of clear vision and hearing plus daily pills and arthritis are no treat. But you know what? Nearing the end of your earthly life only means that you are that much closer to living with Christ in heaven, where it is Christmas all the time.

Don't think of them as failing years—think like a little kid peeking at the Christmas tree, knowing that Christmas is almost here! Remember the angelic message, delivered in a blaze of heavenly light: **"Glory to God in the highest, and on earth peace among those with whom He is pleased!"** (Luke 2:14).

The Christmas message is your life-message: glory for God, peace for you.

Born in a Barn

This morning I visited a new mom in the women's pavilion of a local hospital. What a palace for childbirth! Comfortable and pleasant surroundings, soft music, soft lights, attentive nurses, experienced obstetricians, dazzling arrays of technology ready for every need. There were even handmade knit caps and booties for each new babe. Did I mention the marvelous food?

When the Son of God decided to become the Son of Man, He did not arrive on planet Earth in a women's pavilion. He landed in a barn—a place for animals, not people. The expectant couple apparently was caught by surprise. They had no booties or blankie. Joseph apparently had to tear up his shirt for the first layette.

"While they were there, the time came for [Mary] to give birth. And she gave birth to her firstborn son and wrapped Him in swaddling clothes and laid Him in a manger, because there was no place for them in the inn" (Luke 2:6–7).

The humility of Jesus' birth, chosen by His Father and no accident, sends a powerful message of what He came to do. He came to experience all of our humanity. He came to suffer for us and with us. He was born in a barn so that we could live in His mansion.

December 26

The Father's Heart

What kind of a dad do you have? Is he one that makes you ashamed or one that makes you proud? Some people have to bear the lifelong burden of having an absent father. But good dads provide security, food, and guidance in how to navigate our complex and dangerous world. They show their kids how to be strong, steady, and responsible.

What a priceless gift it is to realize that the God of all has chosen to adopt you as His child, to obligate Himself to rescue you, love you, and protect you. Galatians 3:26 says, **"In Christ Jesus you are all [children] of God, through faith."**

This means the King is your Daddy; that He is not merely watching you, but is working toward your success. It means that when you pray, you don't have to scrape, beg, or tremble. You can speak up with whatever is on your mind, knowing that you are talking to your Father, who loves you very, very much.

December 27

Managing Your Food Intake

God invented food as fuel for human bodily activity, as a part of social events, and to show His goodness by giving it flavor, which brings us no small pleasure.

It's truly amazing, though, to realize how many other uses people have for meals: self-medicating when under stress (nothing makes you forget your troubles like a box of doughnuts), rewarding yourself for hard work or some achievement, showing off, or massaging insecurity by stunning your dinner guests into a food coma.

We could all stand to be more intentional about what we shove down the ol' pie hole. Sometimes we eat out of boredom, social pressure, or just plain sugar cravings. Daniel and his friends chose to be very intentional about their food intake. **"'Test your servants for ten days; let us be given vegetables to eat and water to drink.' . . . At the end of ten days it was seen that they were better in appearance and fatter in flesh than all the youths who ate the king's food"** (Daniel 1:12, 15).

God doesn't demand that you become a vegan. But do think about what you are going to put into your mouth today.

Our bodies aren't really ours to do with as we please. They belong to God because He created us, redeemed us, and made us holy. Although our bodies are going to wear out someday, each day we care for them in a way that says thank you to God for His blessings of both body and soul.

December 28

Getting the Poison Out

It's really hard to trust God when you feel guilt in His presence. Guilt comes on two levels. There's head guilt and heart guilt. In our heads, we know that we have broken God's rules for our behavior. But guilt is also the wretched feelings of shame and failure in our hearts.

Sometimes we let God's Word get us halfway there. We hear the Gospel message and *know* that we have been forgiven, but we don't *feel* forgiven. We still feel dirty; we still feel the intense disappointment we must be to God.

You might think, okay, I know Jesus died for me, but I still feel like such a *fool.* I don't feel worthy of His love, and I can't claim with a straight face to be holy and blameless. The Bible tells us that personal confession is a necessary part of healing the emotional baggage of guilt: **"If we confess our sins, He is faithful and just to forgive us our sins and to cleanse us from all unrighteousness"** (1 John 1:9). Confession is God's way of getting the poisons out. It's like draining a wound. It cuts through all the pretending, denial, and defense.

To get rid of guilt, we first objectively hear what Christ has done for us. And then subjectively, by confessing our sins, saying them out loud to our God without blaming others and without pretending—*then* we will get on the path to emotional healing as well. Our minds will know forgiveness. Our hearts will feel forgiven.

DECEMBER 29

Children Are God's Gifts

Having a child wrenches your life into a completely different direction, doesn't it? A little one seems so helpless and needy. Children take your stuff and break your stuff. They are expensive and exhausting, unappreciative and messy.

What magic the Lord works in the lives of people to whom He gives these little ones! Psalm 127:3 says, **"Children are a heritage from the LORD, the fruit of the womb a reward."** Yep—a *reward!* A sign that He likes you! In spite of the cost, aggravation, and burden, children are truly God's gifts. They bring wonder and innocence, laughter and curiosity, motion and commotion.

Children give us a daily opportunity to love and be loved, surely one of the greatest reasons for being alive. And they love stories about their kind heavenly Father, a risen Savior, and the mysterious Spirit who lives within them.

December 30

Serving People

By nature, the human brain is hardwired for personal gratification. Actually noticing what other people need, caring whether they are okay or not, and bestirring oneself to do something for another are learned behaviors.

They are learned from Christ. The One who washed His disciples' feet one Thursday evening was dead on a cross on Friday afternoon. "I came not to be served, but to serve," He said. It is from Christ that we get not only the example of service above self, but also the energy and the desire to do it.

Paul taught his friends in central Asia Minor (today's Turkey), **"You were called to freedom, brothers. Only do not use your freedom as an opportunity for the flesh, but through love serve one another"** (Galatians 5:13).

It is an absolutely splendid way to spend yourself—your time, your energy, your treasure—to make someone else's life better. Don't begrudge a minute of it.

At the end of all His hard and realistic prophecies, Jesus made two phenomenal promises. The first is that every one of you who hangs onto Christ as Savior will be welcomed into eternal life. You may have lost jobs, wealth, homes, family members, limbs, or health, but if you have Christ, you inherit everything.

These are His incredible words: **"The one who endures to the end will be saved. And this gospel of the kingdom will be proclaimed throughout the whole world as a testimony to all nations, and then the end will come"** (Matthew 24:13–14).

The second promise is a pledge that God won't let the end come until the message of the Savior has reached all over the world. Not only have Christian missionaries entered every country on earth, but shortwave radio, satellite TV, and the Internet can bring the Gospel almost anywhere on the planet. Satan, you lose! In the end, we win!

Special Days

GOOD FRIDAY *Not Guilty*

It is not hard to despise the Pharisees of Jesus' time for their small-minded stupidity, their self-righteous judging of others, and their blindness to their own wretched sin. It is not hard to mock Jesus' disciples as dull-witted fools who usually misunderstood Jesus' mission and agenda. It is not hard today to look around and see evil doers everywhere.

Have you seen the evildoer in the mirror?

The Roman soldiers crucified Christ. The Jewish high council crucified Christ. The Roman legal system, including the governor Pontius Pilate, crucified Christ. Isaiah did too, and so did we. **"He was despised and rejected by men; a man of sorrows, and acquainted with grief; and as one from whom men hide their faces He was despised, and we esteemed Him not"** (Isaiah 53:3).

It is for all those sinful people—and it is for us—that Jesus needed to come to our world to be born, to live perfectly, and to die innocently. It is His sacrifice that makes the blood payment for us. It is His death that enables the Father to say "Not guilty" upon us.

It is by His wounds, His wounds alone, that we are healed.

EASTER *The Real Deal*

By now you have heard just about every kind of sales pitch imaginable. You've been promised everything under the sun. But Easter is the real deal. The resurrection of Jesus really does change everything.

It changes your doubt into confidence. Christ's resurrection absolutely guarantees that His work was successful and acceptable to His Father. Your forgiveness is complete. Easter changes fear into joy. He's alive. Because He lives, you, too, shall live. It changes your mortality into immortality. Christ's resurrection absolutely guarantees that you will depart from your grave by His power. Your casket is now truly a basement bunk bed for a temporary nap *from which you will soon awake* to a life far better than this one.

"Behold! I tell you a mystery. We shall not all sleep, but we shall all be changed, in a moment, in the twinkling of an eye, at the last trumpet. For the trumpet will sound, and the dead will be raised imperishable, and we shall be changed" (1 Corinthians 15:51–52).

Alleluia!

MOTHER'S DAY *Think Like Servants*

Want to infuriate a stay-at-home mother of young children? Ask her when she's going back to work. You're likely to hear, "*Back*? I never stopped!"

Perhaps some women's dream of a great life is easy wealth, days of shopping and travel, unlimited chocolate, and plenty of servants. Maybe God will give you that life. But there is a terrible risk to wealth. You can get so materialistic that you lose your sense of need for a Savior and your gratitude for the Savior you have and what He's done for you.

Hard work is good for the soul. It teaches us to think like servants, doing things for others. It gives a sweet satisfaction of accomplishment that no amount of shopping can match.

Proverbs 31:17–18 celebrates the kind of wife and mother that we all would love to have in our homes: **"She dresses herself with strength and makes her arms strong. She perceives that her merchandise is profitable. Her lamp does not go out at night."** To all the women who work hard to make their homes wonderful places, we bow in appreciation. Thank you.

FATHER'S DAY *A Father's Role*

Have you noticed that all of life is a balancing act? Foolish people can overdo even good and virtuous things—things like eating, working, saving money, and exercising.

Are you a fan of reality TV? You might have seen some shows in which nannies have to straighten out clueless parents who don't know how to parent. Bad fathers are always easy targets. It seems as though TV dads are either spineless softies or stubborn tyrants. There are precious few Bill Cosbys on the air whom we can admire. But we can look to our loving heavenly Father as an example.

Dads, God's goal for your role is the middle way—strong, but not abusive. His Word says, **"Fathers, do not provoke your children, lest they become discouraged"** (Colossians 3:21). Wives and kids absolutely need your strength so that they can feel secure and experience some sense of order. But they also need Dad to show that it's okay to change your mind, apologize, and be tender. Does that make sense? You can be like that.

THANKSGIVING DAY *I'm Thankful*

You know, at this time of year you hear people say things like, "I'm thankful" or "We're grateful." Well, thanking needs a direct object—Thank *whom?*

Sometimes we get confused about where all the good stuff in our lives comes from. We might go along for weeks without giving it any thought. When this happens, it's because we're afflicted with a common problem called GDD (Gratitude Deficit Disorder). St. Paul reminds us where everything comes from: **"He [God] who did not spare His own Son but gave Him up for us all, how will He not also . . . graciously give us all things?"** (Romans 8:32). Not only did our God give us His one and only Son, who is our greatest gift from God—He certainly is able to give us everything else we need.

I encourage you to join me this Thanksgiving Day and every day in making sure that God knows we appreciate Him as the source of everything that is good in our lives—our incomes, the food we eat, our families, our health, everything comes from Him. Be cured of GDD and say, "Thank You, Lord!"

About Pastor Jeske

Pastor Mark Jeske has been bringing the Word of God to viewers of *Time of Grace* since the program began airing in late 2001.

A Milwaukee, Wisconsin, native, Pastor Jeske has served as the senior pastor at St. Marcus Lutheran Church on Milwaukee's near north side since 1980.

Before he began serving as the pastor at St. Marcus, Pastor Jeske spent a year in Colombia, South America, starting a mission church as part of his internship assignment while attending Wisconsin Lutheran Seminary in Mequon, Wisconsin, for his theological postgraduate education. He also spent two years teaching English, history, and Old Testament at Northwestern Preparatory School in Watertown, Wisconsin, prior to his service at St. Marcus.

An accomplished instrumentalist (piano, but also guitar and mandolin, among others), Pastor Jeske enjoys touring with his church's regionally known choir, United Voices of Praise. He especially appreciates jazz, blues, and gospel music.

Pastor Jeske is a serious historian, having studied European, church, and American history for many years. He is passionate about the need for America's various cultures to tolerate, learn from, and truly appreciate one another.

Pastor Jeske has written a Bible commentary on the Bible books James; 1, 2 Peter; 1, 2, 3 John; and Jude (part of *The People's Bible Commentary* series, co-published by Northwestern Publishing House and Concordia Publishing House) and dozens of daily devotional booklets. Numerous articles and booklets based on his recent Sunday messages appear regularly in *Time of Grace* publications.

Pastor Jeske and his wife, Carol, an elementary school teacher, are blessed with four children: John, Sam, Liz, and Michael. They live on the east side of Milwaukee.

Photo credits

January © D. Ciprian-Florin/Shutterstock, Inc.
February © J. Eyre/Shutterstock, Inc.
March © fotoret/Shutterstock, Inc.
April © P. LangeElena Elisseeva/Shutterstock, Inc.
May © E. Elisseeva/Shutterstock, Inc.
June © Frank Jr/Shutterstock, Inc.
July © M,. Bechelli/Shutterstock, Inc.
August © V.J. Matthew/Shutterstock, Inc.
September © E. Elisseeva/Shutterstock, Inc.
October © M.A. Andreevich/Shutterstock, Inc.
November © L. Byerley/Shutterstock, Inc.
December © M. Novak/Shutterstock, Inc.